"Mark McMinn is the rare scholar who can masterfully integrate scientific psychology, Christian theology, *and* counseling practice. In *The Science of Virtue*, he places the best of contemporary positive psychology research in fruitful dialogue with ancient Christian wisdom. McMinn's writings are always intellectually stimulating with fresh insights on important interdisciplinary questions, but it is the practical or formational dimension of his writing that sets his work apart. This book not only contributed to my understanding of key Christian virtues but also gave me clear strategies for practicing the virtues."

—Steven J. Sandage, Boston University

"McMinn has written an important book concerning the compatibility of faith and science. He marries the role of virtuous living with scientific findings and encourages both the church and the academy to cooperate in an effort to help people become all they were created to be. Anyone of faith who counsels people should use this book as a guide to practice and thinking."

—Linda Mintle, Liberty University College
of Osteopathic Medicine

The Science
of Virtue

The Science of Virtue

WHY POSITIVE PSYCHOLOGY MATTERS TO THE CHURCH

Mark R. McMinn

BrazosPress

a division of Baker Publishing Group
Grand Rapids, Michigan

© 2017 by Mark R. McMinn

Published by Brazos Press
a division of Baker Publishing Group
P.O. Box 6287, Grand Rapids, MI 49516-6287
www.brazospress.com

Printed in the United States of America

Library of Congress Cataloging-in-Publication Control Number: 2017021728

ISBN: 978-1-58743-409-9

In keeping with biblical principles of
creation stewardship, Baker Publishing Group advocates the responsible
use of our natural resources. As a
member of the Green Press Initiative, our company uses recycled
paper when possible. The text paper
of this book is composed in part of
post-consumer waste.

17   18   19   20   21   22   23   7   6   5   4   3   2   1

To Auden, Juniper, Eden, Mark, Wesley, and Nash—my six grandchildren.

Stretch toward virtue as you face the joys, suffering, blessings, and pain life will offer you.

Contents

Acknowledgments   xi

Introduction: *A New Conversation about Virtue*   1

1. Wisdom   13

2. Forgiveness   45

3. Gratitude   71

4. Humility   95

5. Hope   121

6. Grace   141

Conclusion: *Let's Work Together*   161

Notes   171

Bibliography   181

Index   189

Acknowledgments

I have been married for thirty-eight years to Lisa, a sociologist, author, and lovely human being. We consider each other to be our "first readers," which means we see those drafts that are not yet ready for anyone else to read and recommend ways to make them better. Once again, Lisa was my first reader for every chapter in this book. She graciously pointed out the best parts and the worst, and helped me find my way forward where my ideas and words were confusing or unclear.

As will be evident in almost every chapter, I am grateful to the John Templeton Foundation for funding a three-year grant that allowed my colleagues, students, and me to study positive psychology and the church. Dr. Nicholas Gibson, the program officer at Templeton who directed this grant, was particularly helpful in reviewing the grant proposal and providing feedback along the way. My colleagues Dr. Rodger Bufford and Dr. MaryKate Morse were collaborators on the grant. Dr. Ward Davis at Wheaton College supervised one of the grant projects. Thanks also to George Fox University and Wheaton College doctoral students who worked on the projects funded by the grant: Andrew Cuthbert, Laura Geczy-Haskins, Paul McLaughlin, Jeff Moody, and Jens Uhder.

I work in a remarkably healthy psychology department, made so in no small part by our department chairperson, Dr. Mary Peterson. My faculty colleagues and doctoral students help me think better than I would without them, and I am thankful for their ongoing role in my professional and spiritual development. Heidi Cuddeford, one of our department's administrative assistants, went well beyond the call of duty to help make the Templeton grant projects successful. Adriana Rangel-Ponce served as an undergraduate assistant who helped with reference citations for the early versions of the manuscript.

The church where I worship each week, Newberg Friends Church, has been part of this project in various ways. Pastors Gregg Koskela and Steve Fawver influenced the curriculum we developed for a wisdom-mentoring program, and the church elders and administrative staff welcomed us to partner with them in running the program. Tamera Brand, Denise and Kevin Brooks, Marcile Crandall, Elaine and Gregg Koskela, Carol and David Sherwood, and Elizabeth and Steve Sherwood all served as capable mentors in the wisdom-mentoring program. Natalie Koskela and Megan Anna Neff both contributed in important ways to the wisdom project as well—in Natalie's case by conducting interviews with wisdom participants and in Megan Anna's case by providing theological insight as we developed the curriculum. The Children of the Light Sunday school class allowed me to teach on each of the chapters in this book and offered helpful feedback along the way.

I also appreciate the pastors and other churches that partnered with us on various projects, including Pastors Jeff Getsinger, Lynn Holt, Jed Maclaurin, Bill Moorman, Rich Miller, Ken Redford, and Andrew Yarborough. Dr. Rebecca Ankeny, former superintendent of the Northwest Yearly Meeting of Friends, was particularly helpful as we established working relationships with churches and pastors.

Finally, I am thankful for the highly professional editorial and design team at Brazos Press. They believed in this idea and helped me craft the manuscript into what it has become.

Introduction

A New Conversation about Virtue

My students look at me funny when I mention 1980, as if we are studying ancient history. It doesn't seem that long ago to me, but most of them were ten years shy of being born. Mount St. Helens erupted that year, gifting my classmates and me with an inch of ash for our college graduation day in Portland, Oregon. Rubik's Cube captured the world's attention and more of my free time than I care to admit. And a concerned couple at my church approached my wife, Lisa, and me a few weeks before we packed our U-Haul for graduate school with a warning that my choice to pursue a doctoral degree in clinical psychology would likely cause us both to abandon our faith. Several weeks later, during my first day on the Vanderbilt University campus, another doctoral student insisted that I couldn't possibly be religious and be a good scientist. Psychology and Christianity were not getting along well in 1980.

While it might not be fair to say that the war between psychology and religion is completely over, I find it remarkable that, thirty-five years later, committed Christians author much of the scientific psychology literature I read. Not only can psychologists be Christians, and Christians be good social scientists, but some of the most thrilling developments in the field have taken place because committed Christians decided to wage peace with psychology.

Much of the change is due to *positive psychology*. In 1998 the president of the American Psychological Association, Martin Seligman, noted that we psychologists had done a very good job describing and treating what goes wrong with people, but had largely overlooked what goes right with people. Almost overnight a vibrant contemporary science of virtue was born,[1] and since then many Christians have been involved in this new movement to study virtue scientifically. Many of the leading researchers on the topic of forgiveness are Christians, as are some of the world's leading experts on gratitude. Almost every scientist currently studying humility is Christian. New research programs are being developed to study grace, and guess who is leading the way? It's difficult to even imagine studying grace without knowing Jesus.

The John Templeton Foundation deserves much of the credit. Even in the face of persistent criticism from old-school scientists who still hold that religion has no place in empirical investigation, the Templeton Foundation has given generously to fund world-class research on religion and science. The foundation demands excellent science while affirming the importance of ultimate questions of meaning and purpose. Many of the Christians involved in positive psychology research, as well as researchers of other religious faiths, have received funding through this foundation.

This is an exhilarating time to be a Christian scholar, a social scientist, a counselor, and a follower of Jesus. Tensions remain between psychology and the church, but mostly they seem as distant as 1980 is to my students. Today we have a new conversation that opens the possibility of partnership and mutual collaboration.

Why Write This Book? Why Read It?

I have four reasons for writing *The Science of Virtue*, but I'm offering just two now and saving two for the end of the introduction.

First, positive psychology helps us to reclaim, or redeem, the language of virtue, which has been largely lost in contemporary times. One understanding of the word "redeem" is to buy back or repurchase something.

Conversations about virtue waned with modernity, as did our ability to comprehend virtue.[2] Today we value science, with its intense scrutiny of "what is," more than virtue, which requires an awareness of who we are to become (teleology). Redeeming virtue requires us to envision a calling, to grasp that we are called to become more fully human, more abundant and Jesus-like. We need a Point B to help make meaning of our current Point A, and then we also need an idea of how to move from Point A to Point B.

Though science cannot fully reclaim the rich understanding of virtue that people had in centuries past, positive psychology is a step in the right direction. Positive psychology is redeeming virtue, bringing topics that have been considered since before the time of Christ—but mostly lost in recent decades—back into focus. As Aristotle taught both virtue ethics and empirical study of the world, so positive psychology brings virtue and science together to consider topics such as hope, resilience, compassion, gratitude, coping, forgiveness, authenticity, humility, creativity, wisdom, and more. I will consider only a few of these topics in a short book such as this, but in each chapter we'll venture into the science of virtue to see how positive psychology is influencing our understanding of human character, mostly in helpful ways.

Mostly. This leads to my second reason for writing the book. Another meaning of the word "redeem" is to change for the better. The contemporary science of virtue will be most effective if the church gets informed and involved. Positive psychology needs the church. I will argue this point in every chapter of the book. In a moment I will summarize my argument for why positive psychology needs the church, but first let me set the context by considering virtue in relation to what Jesus described as the greatest commandments.

Virtue and the Greatest Commandments

Take a minute to think only of yourself. What might you want for your next meal, and how will you go about getting it? Are you enjoying your work? Do you make as much money as you want, and if not, how will you make more? To whom are you attracted, and if that person does not return your affection, how might you go about making that happen? How is your health, and what will make it better? Okay, now it's time to stop, but imagine for a moment that your whole life consisted of thinking only of yourself. This is the essence of vice: self occupying one's entire visual field.

It is tempting to suggest that vice is self-focused and that virtue, in contrast, is other-focused, but being entirely other-focused is not possible for embodied individuals. It seems we are hardwired for self-interest. Consider this sentence: *To be fully virtuous, we should completely empty ourselves of self and focus on the other.* Do you see the logical error? How can a self remove a self? The self exists and will be interested in its own existence. None of us has to work very hard to think about ourselves—that comes quite naturally for us. So the essence of virtue is not to remove a self, or eliminate all self-interest, but to find a balance point where interest of other coexists with interest of self. Further, virtue calls us to consider the growth of the self—both my self and other selves—toward some fully functioning state.

What might I want for my next meal, and how do my food choices affect those who grow my food in my own country and around the world? How do my food choices shape me? How do they affect the character formation of my close and distant neighbors? Am I enjoying my work, and does my work contribute to making the world a more wholesome and beautiful place? How do I balance my interest in money with a profound awareness of those with less access to financial resources? Does my relationship with money reflect a desire to become more and more the person Jesus created me to be? To whom am I attracted, to whom am I committed, and how do my attractions and commitments reflect the sort of love that contributes to the welfare of others? How are my health, the health of those around me, and the health of the planet related? These more complex questions lead to the possibility of virtue, where self-interest is contained and balanced with interest in others and a godly yearning for moral growth. Christian psychologist Everett Worthington writes, "The essence of most virtues is that they self-limit the rights or privileges of the self on behalf of the welfare of others."[3]

Consider the classic virtue of prudence, the ability to choose the right and avoid the wrong. How can we even know what is right without considering how our actions impact others? Prudence requires a balance between self-interest and awareness of the other. Another classic virtue, justice, is to give others what they are due. This requires a cognizance of the other, a keen ability to observe and understand the nature of the other. Fortitude is the strength to be just and prudent, sometimes calling us to put a higher cause above our own self-interest. Temperance calls us to moderate our self-interest, to enjoy the pleasures of this good life without becoming enslaved to them. Virtues limit self-interest, and they call us to become people who routinely do so.

Christian virtue introduces a third dimension—an awareness of and love for God. When the religious leaders of Jesus's day tried to trap him by asking him what was the most important rule from the Old Testament law, Jesus gave an answer that has been resounding for over two millennia: "'You must love the LORD your God with all your heart, all your soul, and all your mind.' This is the first and greatest commandment. A second is equally important: 'Love your neighbor as yourself.' The entire law and all the demands of the prophets are based on these two commandments" (Matt. 22:37–40). Here we see that following Jesus involves loving God, loving the other, and properly managing our instinctive desire to love ourselves. We may sing catchy praise choruses about worship being all about Jesus, but actually it's not. Jesus clearly connected loving God with love of self and other, and so collective worship is about honoring a relational God who cares deeply about each of us. Worship is a virtuous act involving God, self, the other who sits beside us, and the other who lives across the world.

Balancing an awareness of God and other with our natural desire to honor ourselves calls us to a more complex set of questions. What do I want for my next meal, and how do my food choices reflect both a love for local and global neighbors and a desire to understand and love what God loves? How does my work reveal God's image and contribute to God's redemptive presence in our broken world? How do my relationships image God while bringing joy, meaning, and hope both to the other and myself?

We can categorize vice, virtue, and Christian virtue if we wish. Many helpful taxonomies have been developed over the centuries, from the seven deadly sins that were actually eight until Pope Gregory the Great distilled the list a bit in the sixth century, to the four cardinal virtues that made their way into Christian thinking through Aristotle, to the three theological virtues identified by the apostle Paul in 1 Corinthians 13. But all of these taxonomies ultimately reveal that vice elevates self to preeminence and traps us in gratifying present desires. In contrast, virtue calls us to a place of balance where we exercise control over wanton self-interest because we love God and neighbor. Virtue invites us to imagine a better self and a better world, and Christian virtue does this while being embedded in a profound love relationship with God.

Why Positive Psychology Needs the Church

With this understanding of virtue, now we can explore the essence of the argument I make throughout this book. Left to itself, psychology tends to veer toward self-interest. Many have written scathing critiques of psychology, some of which border on the ridiculous, but one of the most thoughtful and compelling critiques is offered by psychologist Paul Vitz in his text *Psychology as Religion: The Cult of Self-Worship*,[4] where he explores the ubiquity of selfism in contemporary society. Psychology can become a worldview, much as a religion, according to Vitz, and can lead to an excessive focus on the self. Even positive psychology, which developed after Vitz's book was published, can veer in this direction.

Consider forgiveness, which has been an enormous boon to the positive psychology movement. Not too many decades ago forgiveness was relegated to religion and was almost never considered in the context of psychology. Now we have thousands of articles on the topic, including impressive scientific studies showing the power of forgiveness (more on this in chapter 2). But find someone on the street and ask why forgiveness is important, and you're likely to hear about the immediate personal benefits of forgiveness. Indeed, much of the science demonstrates the personal health benefits of forgiving an offender. Do you want to lower your blood pressure, to sleep better, to feel happier? Forgive someone who has hurt you. This is important research that should be celebrated, but notice how easily this can veer toward focus on the self and on a static view of self.

Now consider forgiveness from the vantage point of Christian virtue, as we will in detail in chapter 2. It's not just about me wanting to get on with my life and feel better. No, forgiveness is a spiritual act, a worshipful act, in recognition of God's gracious and forgiving character. God's character, revealed in Jesus, changes me. To whatever extent I am changed, I can then have a transforming effect on others around me, helping them glimpse what it looks like to move more toward the life Jesus lives. Thus conceived, forgiveness is a community act, designed to foster healing, hope, and growth.[5] We forgivers need the church to remind us why it matters, to put our self-interest in the context of something deeper and richer than we naturally might consider.

Stanton Jones, former provost of Wheaton College, offers a useful and balanced critique of positive psychology.[6] While Jones acknowledges various dimensions to be celebrated, he also raises serious concerns about how positive psychology understands the nature of existence (ontology), knowledge (epistemology), and practical philosophy. This is not just academic quibbling; it is the necessary role of Christian scholars to consider how any new scientific advance squares with Christianity. As much as I value the past twenty years of positive psychology, the movement is still in its infancy. The church has been around a long time and serves as a custodian of truth. Positive psychology needs the church in order to identify its strengths and blind spots. I've given a preview of this by considering forgiveness and will make similar arguments about wisdom (chapter 1), gratitude (chapter 3), humility (chapter 4), hope (chapter 5), and grace (chapter 6).

Why the Church Needs Positive Psychology

I reserved my final two reasons for writing this book until the end of this introduction, knowing that one is controversial and the other quite challenging. Here's the controversial one: the church can benefit from positive psychology. One could argue that the church is relatively self-sustaining, has been over many centuries, and has little need for the latest psychological trend or current social-science research. Still, I write this book because I am convinced the church needs to consider positive psychology and what it offers to conversations about virtue that have been going on for centuries. I offer two illustrations of this point here and will suggest more in following chapters.

One reason the church needs positive psychology is that the time has come for Christianity and science to become better friends. Consider the plight of a teenager growing up in a church that avoids dialogue with science. On Sunday this teenager learns that religion is the path to truth, and perhaps even that science is not to be trusted. Monday through Friday, in the context of a public school, the teenager learns that science is the most credible way to know something, and perhaps that religion is backward and naïve. At some point in life this teenager will face a choice to remain in the church and distrust science or to trust science and leave the church. Increasingly, the church is losing this battle. We may hear something like this and blame public school systems, but what are we doing to promote meaningful dialogue and peacemaking between science and faith? Social and natural scientists at any Christian college will affirm that science and faith are good conversation partners and need not be foes, but sometimes the church gives a different message. Embracing meaningful dialogue between science and faith will help build the church and keep us relevant in a time when science is garnering even more credit than it deserves. Positive psychology provides an ideal venue to foster conversation between science and faith because the subject matter—virtue—is something valued by both parties in the conversation. We may go about studying virtue differently, but we both care about it deeply and are looking for truth.

Another reason that the church needs positive psychology is to make the tenets of Christian thought practical. Consider forgiveness again. Most Christians agree that forgiveness is important. Jesus taught that we should forgive others in various ways, even right in the middle of the Lord's Prayer. All through the New Testament we see some mysterious relationship between God forgiving us and us forgiving others. Most of us have heard many sermons about the topics and feel both an obligation to forgive and peace when it happens. But how do we forgive? What are the practical steps I can take to forgive someone who has wounded me deeply? The practical strategies for accomplishing forgiveness tend not to show up in the Bible, though it is clear that we are called to figure it out. I have good news about this because positive psychologists have done tremendous work in figuring out the mechanism of forgiveness. Imagine a sermon that goes beyond the Christian mandate to forgive and demonstrates how it is actually done. Likely, that will be a sermon by a pastor who understands both Christian theology and positive psychology.

Christian Counselors and Positive Psychology

Finally, I offer the reason for writing the book that is most challenging, and likely most rewarding: positive psychology can help

Christian counselors and pastoral counselors do their work in new and refreshing ways. Why is this so challenging? Because the two related branches of psychology—clinical psychology on the one hand, and positive psychology on the other—haven't built many bridges for meaningful interaction. Clinical and counseling psychologists meet with their patients and clients and offer services based on traditional theories of intervention, whether they be psychodynamic, cognitive-behavioral, family focused, client centered, or some related strain. Meanwhile, positive psychologists tend to work in the academy. Though many positive psychologists are trained in clinical work, they tend to keep their research quite separate from their work with patients. With the exception of forgiveness (chapter 2), gratitude (chapter 3), and some preliminary work on humility, positive psychology stays in the ivory tower too often, and it seems important to ponder its implications for the work of Christian counselors.

As a clinical psychologist who has been immersed in the Christian counseling movement for many years through reading, counseling, researching, speaking, and writing, I think it responsible to speculate a bit at the end of each chapter about how positive psychology can inform Christian counselors. So I will.

In summary, I offer four reasons to read this book: because it is worth knowing something about positive psychology, because positive psychology needs the church, because the church needs positive psychology, and because positive psychology can help Christian counselors think creatively about their work. If this all seems somewhat vague now, it will become clearer as we move into chapters about particular virtues: wisdom, forgiveness, gratitude, humility, hope, and grace. And if grace doesn't seem like a virtue that belongs on this list, try to suspend judgment on that for now. I'll address why I include grace as a virtue later.

The married couple in our church that warned Lisa and me about the dangers of psychology back in 1980 were two of the most godly and honorable people I have ever known. They loved Jesus and lived out virtue in remarkable ways. As difficult as it was going against their advice, I think Lisa and I have also found important ways to love God and neighbor in the process. Psychology has changed me, especially positive psychology, and some years later, when Lisa completed a PhD in sociology, that changed her as well, but in the process we have grown comfortable with the idea that social science can enhance our faith just as faith can sharpen our science. Join me on this integrative journey, and let's work together to redeem virtue.

1

······

Wisdom

The day before I started this chapter I played flag football with some of my doctoral students. Though I am thirty years their senior, I tried my best to keep up for three hours of great fun. Today my sore muscles scream any time I try to move. My wife, Lisa, would say they are reprimanding me for my foolishness. Typing on the keyboard is about the only motion that doesn't hurt. It seems both fitting and paradoxical to begin writing about wisdom the morning after punishing my body in the name of a good time. Hopefully I haven't just destroyed any credibility I have on the topic.

Football is a small example, but doesn't it seem we need vast amounts of wisdom to understand and participate well in contemporary life? Picture concentric circles, starting with individual choices and extending outward to our memberships and civic responsibilities. In each of these circles we yearn for wisdom. Individually, we continually confront questions about how to best use our time in an age when consumerism and entertainment demand our continual attention. We make choices about education, training for careers, choosing careers, changing careers, and retiring from careers. How should we earn, spend, and give our money? If we have too much to do, and likely we do, then how should we balance sleep, leisure, work, and domestic chores? And why do we keep misplacing our phones and keys at the most inconvenient times? How are we going to lose a few pounds, and how much does it matter that we do? Is this just a third glass of wine, or is it a drinking problem? Am I reading a legitimate email or another scam? Should I even open the attachment, and if I do will it install a virus on my computer?

Moving outward on these concentric circles, many of us exist in family units that call for yet another level of wisdom. Honoring parents, loving a partner well, keeping children safe in a complex and violent world while raising them to be kind and compassionate, creating a balance of closeness without becoming overly enmeshed, knowing when to set rules and how many to set with adolescent children. Who purchases and prepares the food? How can we make ends meet in financially lean times?

Many live in small communities, with friends and neighbors who may delight or annoy us, or both. When do we set boundaries, and when are we just being selfish? Do we reach out to our friends and neighbors when we're in need, or do we manage things on our own? How do we respond when others reach out to us with their needs? Some of us are part of church communities where we have to decide how important ideological and doctrinal differences are in relation to unity in Christ. Because many churches are dwindling these days, we face a host of questions about how to stay relevant in a postmodern world and when efforts to be relevant cross over to moral compromise.

Stepping back to see the larger concentric circles, we see that we belong to civic groups, whether city, state, nation, or world. Making sense of our voting rights and responsibilities and knowing how to prioritize candidates' views on issues of personal morality, national security, economics, and social justice are no easy tasks. To whom do we offer our charitable giving when our resources are finite and the local and global needs seem infinite? Everywhere we turn, every day we live, we are people longing for wisdom in a complex world.

Social scientists have been studying wisdom, which is good news to some, irrelevant to others, and perhaps bad news to the science skeptics. As one who has spent my career valuing contributions of science, I aim to foster a relationship between what science helps us discover and what faith has long told us about wisdom. By putting science and faith side by side and letting them influence each other, we can construct wisdom for daily living.

The Science of Wisdom

One of last night's flag football players, Paul McLaughlin, walked into my office three years ago, announcing that he wanted to do a dissertation on wisdom. "That's a great topic," I said, "but psychologists don't really study wisdom." Paul went to the library and proved me wrong. It turns out psychologists have been studying wisdom for at least three decades now. Much of the work has come out of the University of Chicago and the Max Planck Institute for Human Development in Berlin. I've read quite a lot about wisdom over the past three years, Paul and I published a paper on the topic, and Paul completed his dissertation on wisdom.[1]

Sometimes I look enviously at chemists and imagine that the constructs they study have clear definitions based on numbers of carbon molecules and the types of bonds they share. I'm probably wrong about the simplicity of chemistry, but still I can't imagine a more difficult construct to define than wisdom. If we asked a hundred people to define wisdom, we would likely get a vast array of perspectives, ranging from shrewd financial advice to spiritual practices to a decision-making model for whom to marry (and whom never to marry).

Paul Baltes, a world-renowned expert on developmental psychology and founder of the Berlin Wisdom Project, considered wisdom to be "expert-level knowledge in the fundamental pragmatics

of life."[2] Note that wisdom involves knowledge, but is not the same
as knowledge. You may know immense amounts of information
about healthy living, but if you neglect the fundamental pragmatics of eating well, exercising, sleeping, and experiencing joy in
the present moment, then your knowledge will not be of much
benefit. Wisdom goes beyond knowledge by applying knowledge
to the pragmatics of living well.

Yale psychologist Robert Sternberg makes a similar argument
that knowledge must be applied in order for wisdom to show up,
but reminds us that this is not just about self-interest: "Wisdom
is involved when practical intelligence is applied to maximizing
not just one's own or someone else's self-interest, but rather a
balance of various self-interests (intrapersonal) with the interests
of others (interpersonal) and of other aspects of the context in
which one lives (extrapersonal), such as one's city or country or
environment or even God."[3]

Knowledge itself isn't enough. We probably all know relational
experts who struggle in their own intimate relationships. Perhaps
they are pastors or counselors or psychologists with a vast amount
of knowledge on how we should relate to others, but they struggle
with practical ways of applying their knowledge in maintaining
close, lasting relationships. Wisdom requires both knowledge and
pragmatic application of that knowledge, and it extends beyond
our self and into the realm of caring about others.

I recognize that these definitions of wisdom may not fully satisfy
Christians, philosophers, or those who are generally suspicious of
scientists, but let's stay here for a while before moving to a more
nuanced Christian understanding of wisdom.

Because science involves measurable criteria, it is not enough
to simply define wisdom as expert-level knowledge in the fundamental pragmatics of life. We need something more specific and
measurable. Scholars at the Berlin Wisdom Project articulated and
tested five criteria that fit within their definition: factual knowledge,
procedural knowledge, life-span contextualism, values relativism,
and managing uncertainty.[4] The first two—factual and procedural

knowledge—are considered basic criteria in that they reflect the knowledge necessary for wisdom, but they are not sufficient in themselves. The remaining three criteria are about the pragmatic application of knowledge to a particular situation.

These five criteria can be illustrated with a silly story, though the silliness won't be clear until the story is done. Many years ago our pet cat, Frisky, ran away when we agreed to dog-sit for a few days. Frisky "belonged" to my daughter Sarah, though it seems reasonable to question whether a cat can actually belong to anyone. We assumed Frisky was just hanging out in the woods around our house and that he would return at the conclusion of our three-day dog-sitting stint, but he didn't. Ten days passed, and then one day after work Lisa told me that she saw Frisky lying dead on the side of the road on her way home from graduate school.

The first part of wisdom is *factual knowledge*. When we didn't know Frisky's whereabouts, we didn't have many options for moving forward in wisdom. But now, with Lisa's revelation, we had factual knowledge, and we needed to figure out how to be wise. Our daughter's beloved cat was dead, and she didn't know.

The next part of wisdom is *procedural knowledge*. When X happens, Y is the best thing to do. Procedure knowledge comes with time and experience. Because I was raised on a farm where we would have never considered having an indoor pet, I was quite uninformed about procedural knowledge when it comes to dead pets. Lisa, who was raised with one or more dogs in her home, knew much more in this regard. She helped me understand that the best thing to do when one's pet dies on the road is to bring it home and bury it. So on that rainy autumn evening, after our three daughters were in bed, Lisa and I went and found Frisky, put his body in a cardboard box, dug a hole under a big Douglas fir tree, and buried him. I'm sure some would say the best procedural knowledge would be to show Sarah Frisky's dead body and let her hold him once more before the burial, though that wouldn't have worked out well in this case because Frisky wasn't very presentable or even clearly recognizable due to the work of maggots—a point that becomes relevant later on.

Sarah was in early elementary school at the time and was (and always has been) a sensitive soul who sees pain in others and experiences her own pain deeply. We knew that telling her about Frisky would affect her profoundly. We also knew that this would not be the last time she experienced loss and pain. Part of wisdom is *life-span contextualism*—recognizing that each of us is living out a story with a past, present, and future. We had no idea at the time that Sarah would someday confront the unwanted failure of a nine-year marriage, with two young children at home. All we knew was that Frisky's death would be a huge loss and that more losses lay ahead. We had to tell her.

The fourth criterion for wisdom is *values relativism*. This is not a sloppy pluralism, but rather the notion that most tough decisions involve competing values. In this case, we would have loved to shield Sarah from pain, which is an honorable value for parents to hold. Parents often endure hardships for the sake of their children. At the same time, we value honesty and see the importance of open, candid conversation with our children. These values competed, but Lisa and I knew that it was best to let Sarah know what happened to Frisky and to allow Sarah the pain of her grief. We flanked either side of her bed as we told her the story, and then each of us held her hand or touched her shoulder as she sobbed and writhed in pain.

The final criterion is *managing uncertainty*. Wisdom requires us to stop short of answers sometimes and to be willing to confront the paradoxes, mysteries, and unknown dimensions of living. Sarah certainly faced her share of uncertainty in the days that followed, and it turns out that Lisa and I did too.

Several days after the burial, Lisa and I were playing cards with some friends in the living room when our youngest daughter, Megan Anna, bounded into the room and pronounced, "Mom, Dad, Frisky's back!" We assured her that Frisky was dead and that he couldn't come back, but at her repeated insistence we

SIDEBAR 1.1

Scientific Wisdom in Action

Here is a scenario that comes from wisdom science: a fourteen-year-old girl wants to get married. What would you think and say?

It is probably tempting to blurt out a loud "NO!" But hold on a minute. Let's consider this based on the five wisdom criteria coming from the Berlin Wisdom Project.

Factual Knowledge

We'll want to know something about the girl. Does she live in contemporary times? What is her cultural background? If she is a girl from Nazareth who lived a couple thousand years ago, we may have a different perspective than if she is a girl from Boston in the twenty-first century.

Procedural Knowledge

What sort of goals does this girl have in wanting to get married? How much time does she have to make the decision? Does she live in a time and place where marriage is more about function or more about romance, and if about romance, does she love the person she is considering marrying? Does she have wise mentors in her life that will help her make this decision, or is she in a position of deciding by herself?

Life-Span Contextualism

Is there a reason she is trying to escape her current living situation, such as an abusive home or living in poverty? Would marriage be likely to help her overcome difficult life circumstances, or would it simply add more difficulty?

Values Relativism

What are her priorities in marriage? How do her personal priorities mesh with the larger social good? What sort of universal values related to the good of self, others, and society should be considered?

Managing Uncertainty

To what extent is the girl prepared to deal with the uncertainty of her future? To what extent are you as an advice giver prepared to do the same? How can she prepare for an uncertain future even as she makes a decision about whether to marry?

went out to the back porch and, sure enough, there was Frisky, skinnier than usual, but definitely Frisky. Apparently we buried someone else's dead cat.

The happy conclusion is why I call this a silly story, but life consists of hundreds of these stories—some of them with happy endings and some without. Here, in the midst of life's stories, we strive to find expert-level knowledge in the fundamental pragmatics of life as we grow toward wisdom.

More remains to be discussed about the science of wisdom, but first it is worth considering what Christianity has to say about the topic. If we are to redeem wisdom, it will involve both appreciating the science of wisdom and considering how faith enriches our understanding of it.

Moving toward a Christian View of Wisdom

After Paul convinced me there is a science of wisdom, we started planning his dissertation, a task that was assisted by a grant from the John Templeton Foundation. Some colleagues and I had just been granted funds to promote positive psychology in the church, including funding for five doctoral dissertations. Paul and I brainstormed about an ideal local church for his project, then set up a meeting with several church leaders at a nearby underground restaurant. Subterra Restaurant isn't a secret-society sort of eatery, but it is literally underground. It happens to be one of the best places for group conversation and good food in our little town of Newberg, Oregon.

After some initial conversation, Paul tossed out the definition of wisdom I have just been describing: "Wisdom is expert-level knowledge in the fundamental pragmatics of life." His words were met with silence that seemed difficult to interpret. Then the questions started coming. Should wisdom be so tightly linked to knowledge? Is experience being discounted here? Can wisdom be adequately defined in such nonrelational terms? What about encounter with the living God? We were in for a lively conversation, and an important one.

Gregg Koskela, the lead pastor of Newberg Friends Church, offered another perspective on wisdom—one deeply embedded in a Christian worldview: "Wisdom comes from the history of regular individual and corporate practices that lead to making decisions in line with the character of Christ." Thus understood, wisdom is relational, spiritual, and developed over years of practice. It's reminiscent of that oft-repeated notion in Scripture that the fear of God is the beginning of wisdom.

Note that the scientific definition that Paul and I offered is not mutually exclusive with Gregg's faith-based description of wisdom. Gregg's words speak to how wisdom is developed, whereas our scientific definition describes the outcome of wisdom. Science and faith can work together here, and both can enrich our understanding of wisdom.

Paul and I ventured forward with his wisdom project in the church that Gregg pastored. I'll tell you about our results later, but first I should mention something we learned from MaryKate Morse, a professor at George Fox Seminary and a member of Paul's dissertation committee. Morse's PhD in organizational leadership involved writing her dissertation on wisdom, so it seemed a natural choice to have her on the committee. In the process of reviewing Paul's dissertation proposal, she informed us of a distinction that theologians make between *conventional* and *critical* wisdom. Paul has a master's degree in theology, so he was somewhat familiar with this. I love theology, but because I am not formally trained, I had never heard of this distinction between conventional and critical wisdom. Paul and I each read Morse's very long (and very good) dissertation and learned a great deal in the process.

Conventional wisdom is best viewed as commonsense guidelines for living the good life. In many ways it is quite similar to the scientific views of wisdom discussed earlier in this chapter— expert knowledge in the fundamental pragmatics of life. If you

---

The Surprising Wisdom of Jesus

Jesus didn't offer wisdom from a throne, as King Solomon did in the Old Testament. Instead, the wisdom of Jesus reveals the unexpected, mysterious ways of God's relentless love (1 Cor. 2:7). Rather than coming as a triumphant ruler, Jesus—God incarnate—came as a baby born in a smelly barn.

This is the surprising Jesus who changed the world forever. People expected a politically powerful Messiah, and they got a carpenter and an itinerant minister who lived in the lowliest of conditions and ultimately humbled himself to the point of death by crucifixion (Phil. 2:5–11).

Throughout the New Testament we see the surprising wisdom of Jesus as he confronts prevailing assumptions. It's a costly wisdom, stirring up traditional assumptions and causing dissension among the religious leaders of the day. And when this controversial sort of wisdom led to its natural conclusion and the leaders of the day came to arrest Jesus in the garden, then Jesus healed his accuser's ear after Peter chopped it off.

Borrowing from Henri Nouwen's (2007) book title, here's to "the selfless way of Christ: downward mobility and the spiritual life."*

Healing on the Sabbath

"One Sabbath day as Jesus was teaching in a synagogue, he saw a woman who had been crippled by an evil spirit. She had been bent double for eighteen years and was unable to stand up straight. When Jesus saw her, he called her over and said, 'Dear woman, you are healed of your sickness!' Then he touched her, and instantly she could stand straight. How she praised God!

"But the leader in charge of the synagogue . . ." (Luke 13:10–14)

---

read through the Old Testament proverbs, you are mostly reading conventional wisdom.

But we all know that conventional wisdom must sometimes be questioned and reconsidered. Jesus was a radical insofar as he questioned a number of the religious rules of his day. The devout religious leaders had their systems of wisdom in place, and Jesus challenged many of them, even to the point of being labeled a

Wisdom

23

Teaching the Paradoxes

"What blessings await you when people hate you and exclude you and mock you and curse you as evil because you follow the Son of Man. When that happens, be happy! Yes, leap for joy! For a great reward awaits you in heaven. And remember, their ancestors treated the ancient prophets that same way." (Luke 6:22–23)

Hanging Out with Sinners

"Later, Levi invited Jesus and his disciples to his home as dinner guests, along with many tax collectors and other disreputable sinners. (There were many people of this kind among Jesus' followers.) But when the teachers of religious law who were Pharisees saw him eating with tax collectors and other sinners, they asked his disciples, 'Why does he eat with such scum?'

"When Jesus heard this, he told them, 'Healthy people don't need a doctor—sick people do.'" (Mark 2:15–17)

Verging on Sacrilege

"So if you are presenting a sacrifice at the altar in the Temple and you suddenly remember that someone has something against you, leave your sacrifice there at the altar. Go and be reconciled to that person. Then come and offer your sacrifice to God." (Matt. 5:23–24)

I love being surprised by Jesus. His is a wisdom that turns things upside down in order to remind us how to love God and neighbor, and how deeply God loves us.

*Henri J. M. Nouwen, *The Selfless Way of Christ: Downward Mobility and the Spiritual Life* (London: Orbis, 2007).

blasphemer and sentenced to death. Throughout the Sermon on the Mount Jesus repeated, "You have heard it said . . . but I say to you." He rocked the boat. Based on Gospel accounts, it appears that Jesus did more healing on the Sabbath than any other day. I wonder why. Could one of his reasons have been that he wanted people to rethink the prevailing wisdom of the day—a calcified sort of wisdom that had led to rigid and oppressive rules? Maybe

Jesus deliberately mixes up people's understanding of virtuous living.

A second kind of wisdom—critical wisdom—is also found in the Bible, especially in Ecclesiastes, Job, and the life of Jesus. Critical wisdom is often countercultural, always discerning, and sometimes mysterious. Folks with critical wisdom think outside the box, but not just for the sake of being unconventional; they think differently because of a profound commitment to justice and goodness. It's difficult to capture this sort of wisdom with words, and it certainly can't be contained in simple proverbs about how to live the good life.

Consider the wisdom poem in Job 28, where Job ponders the deep mysteries of wisdom, so elusive and intangible.

> "But do people know where to find wisdom?
>   Where can they find understanding?
> It is hidden from the eyes of all humanity.
>   Even the sharp-eyed birds in the sky cannot
>   discover it.
> Destruction and Death say,
>   'We've heard only rumors of where wisdom
>   can be found.'
>
> "God alone understands the way to wisdom;
>   he knows where it can be found,
> for he looks throughout the whole earth
>   and sees everything under the heavens.
> He decided how hard the winds should blow
>   and how much rain should fall.
> He made the laws for the rain
>   and laid out a path for the lightning.
> Then he saw wisdom and evaluated it.
>   He set it in place and examined it thoroughly.
> And this is what he says to all humanity:
> 'The fear of the Lord is true wisdom;
>   to forsake evil is real understanding.'"
>
> Job 28:20–28

Ponder the paradoxical wisdom in the book of Ecclesiastes, where the author begins with the shocking and rather dismal assertion that "everything is meaningless" (1:2), then follows with twelve chapters of ironies and uncertainties. Interestingly, the author concludes with the same conclusion as Job: "Fear God and obey his commands" (12:13).

At some risk of heresy, here are some faux Bible verses to illustrate the difference between conventional and critical wisdom. Knowing what we now know about the health effects of antioxidants and the taste of dark chocolate, one might imagine a proverb such as: "Eat dark chocolate, for it is good." Realistically, we might want to add one clause on the end: "Eat dark chocolate, for it is good. But not too much." One might even imagine a verse like this in the biblical proverbs, because it reads like common sense, helping us navigate the pragmatics of life. This is conventional wisdom.

But now consider what Jesus might say if he were discussing dark chocolate. I can imagine a statement such as this in the Sermon on the Mount: "You have heard the proverb that says, 'Eat dark chocolate,' but I say to you it is better to eat no chocolate at all than to eat chocolate that contributes to human oppression." In this Jesus would be affirming conventional wisdom—it's still good to eat dark chocolate for health-related reasons and to celebrate the goodness of life—but at the same time Jesus would push against the cultural mindlessness of the day, being profoundly aware of and deeply troubled by the human atrocities committed in the name of supplying cheap chocolate to industrialized countries.[5]

The prophet Isaiah spoke of the incisive wisdom of Jesus hundreds of years before he showed up in swaddling clothes, and though today's chocolate trade is not mentioned, it is certainly implicated.

> And the Spirit of the LORD will rest on him—
>   the Spirit of wisdom and understanding,
> the Spirit of counsel and might,
> the Spirit of knowledge and the fear of the LORD.

He will delight in obeying the LORD.
  He will not judge by appearance
  nor make a decision based on hearsay.
He will give justice to the poor
  and make fair decisions for the exploited.
The earth will shake at the force of his word,
  and one breath from his mouth will destroy the wicked.
He will wear righteousness like a belt
  and truth like an undergarment.

                                                    Isa. 11:2–5

Jesus, the perfect image of God, is the master of critical wisdom. He didn't come to abolish conventional wisdom but to enliven it, to flesh out the greatest commandments of loving God and loving neighbor as self, to remind us of life's deep mystery, to call us back to the fear and awe of God when we so easily settle for a religion composed of cognitive beliefs and behavioral lists that make us feel holier than others.

If we are to become wise, we need to be willing to stand against social tides, but not for the sake of being nonconformists or to be noticed for being countercultural. This is about finding the moral courage to do what is right, to love mercy, and to walk humbly with God (Mic. 6:8) even when it means questioning the prevailing practices of the day, such as buying cheap chocolate.

Wisdom's Telos

One example of critical wisdom can be found in considering the idea of *telos* in an age when the concept has been largely lost. *Telos*, a Greek word, refers to an end purpose or goal, the full picture of our moral and physical capacities, intentions, and capability. If we could imagine a fully whole human living a thriving, abundant life, then we would be picturing something like telos. We are inclined to equate full functioning with popular opinion, notoriety, or financial success, but this is not adequate to understand telos.

It's more about finding the natural and purposeful end of what it means to be fully human. An acorn grows into a majestic oak tree and finds its telos, and a human may grow into a fully functioning person, revealing what humans are for. Christians see Jesus as the perfect exemplar of telos.

Telos is so difficult to keep in focus amidst a consumerist society. In my early career I criticized older friends who seemed to think and talk excessively about the stock market. It seemed trite compared to my desire to change the world. But now, as my own retirement looms and I have abandoned hope of changing the world overly much, I find myself eyeing 401(k) balances and stock market growth, wondering what sort of financial security lies ahead. The humbling truth is that I am prone to do what people in our day do—look to money as my source of security in the future and accomplishment in life. Then I remember the words of James: "Look here, you who say, 'Today or tomorrow we are going to a certain town and will stay there a year. We will do business there and make a profit.' How do you know what your life will be like tomorrow? Your life is like the morning fog—it's here a little while, then it's gone" (James 4:13–14). What if financial growth receded into the background and I focused instead on telos growth for whatever time I have left? I wonder what it would be like to grow 6 percent each year toward the fully alive, abundant living that Jesus calls me to.

Virtue requires a vision of what is possible, replete with a deep understanding of our purposes for living, and then movement toward that telos. Maybe we should put this on our quarterly reports, rather than what we audaciously call "net worth."

In a world that looks to money for net worth, we assume wisdom is found in business acumen, shrewdness, being competitive when needed, knowing how to get ahead. But wisdom in God's economy looks different. The book of James offers a glimpse of this contrast:

> For jealousy and selfishness are not God's kind of wisdom. Such things are earthly, unspiritual, and demonic. For wherever there

is jealousy and selfish ambition, there you will find disorder and evil of every kind.

But the wisdom from above is first of all pure. It is also peace loving, gentle at all times, and willing to yield to others. It is full of mercy and the fruit of good deeds. It shows no favoritism and is always sincere. And those who are peacemakers will plant seeds of peace and reap a harvest of righteousness. (James 3:15–18)

Here is a picture of a fully functioning person—one who loves peace, lives gently, embodies humility, is full of mercy, loves to do good, and refuses to play favorites. This telos helps us to understand a Christian view of wisdom.

Scientific and Christian Wisdom, Side by Side

The purpose of this book, and of much of my career, is to propose a sort of partnership between science and the church. Science can inform us regarding wisdom, but it has its limits. Christianity plumbs the depth of wisdom, but we can still benefit from science to keep faith humble.

First, consider a limitation of science and why Christian faith can help. Science needs parsimony. We scientists take complicated constructs and scrub them down so they can be pristine and measurable. Sadly, in the process we sometimes change the very construct we set out to study in the first place. If we take a construct as complex as wisdom and brush off all the religious and spiritual "contaminants" so that we can measure it effectively with people who may or may not be religious, might we be left with something that is no longer recognizable as wisdom within a faith community? I fear we may have done this with forgiveness also, but I'll save that for a later chapter. Science needs faith in order to remind us why these constructs we study have meaning and importance and to keep their rich nuance in perspective. Nowhere in the scientific literature do I find mention of conventional and critical wisdom, yet it seems so important for a full-bodied understanding of the construct.

But faith alone has its limits also. So much about wisdom is discovered in Scripture and through centuries of Christian thought, but some of it needs to be tested so that we're not merely accepting what we have been taught without critical appraisal. Just as the apostle Paul suggested that prophecies ought to be tested and sifted for the good (1 Thess. 5:21), so the teachings of the church will be better if they hold up under scrutiny. For example, if we ask ten churchgoing Christians about the relationship between age and wisdom, we will probably hear from nine or all ten of them that wisdom increases with age. This is not explicitly taught in the Bible, but has become part of our wisdom tradition—we assume it grows with life experience. It turns out that wisdom doesn't change as much as we think over the life span. Studies in Japan[6] and Germany[7] show wisdom staying almost constant after the age of thirty. In the United States, wisdom continues growing throughout adulthood, but it's not because we're wiser than folks in Japan or Germany. To the contrary, the average thirty-year-old in Japan is already as wise as the average fifty-five-year-old in the United States.[8] Could it be that wisdom comes faster in a culture that reveres those who are older? In the United States we tend to cherish youth over aging, and perhaps one cost of this is youthful folly.

The surprising finding that wisdom doesn't increase much with adult aging, at least among samples of Germans and Japanese, is coupled with a finding that it increases dramatically between the ages of thirteen and twenty-five. In psychology we often talk about critical developmental windows. These windows are particular times in life when monumental changes take place. Most children learn to walk in their second year of life. They also begin speaking words around the same time. A few years later they engage in monumental shifts in cognitive development—they start realizing that the events of life are not fully contained in and constrained by their personal perceptions. From the limited research available, it appears that ages thirteen to twenty-five represent a sort of critical window for the development of wisdom.

Wisdom Goes to Church

In light of this critical window for wisdom development, my doctoral student Paul set out to study whether a church-based mentoring program would promote wisdom among young adults, ages eighteen to twenty-five. We started by developing a curriculum for eight small-group mentoring meetings. To be an effective partnership, this had to be a collaborative process, involving both Paul and me as social scientists, as well as the church leaders.

Remember Pastor Gregg's description of wisdom from our lunch meeting? *Wisdom comes from the history of regular individual and corporate practices that lead to making decisions in line with the character of Christ.* Gregg later developed this further by suggesting three steps toward wisdom.

1. Experiencing God through a variety of spiritual practices (Scripture, prayer, silence)
2. Considering one's own experience in the context of trusting relationships with others who share common core values (small-group conversation with leaders and peers)
3. Understanding, adapting, and appropriating the values and practices that have become a vital part of a particular Christian community (discerning what wisdom looks like in this situation)

Paul and I started with Gregg's understanding of wisdom, coupled it with the theological notion of critical wisdom discussed earlier, and developed the first draft of a wisdom-mentoring curriculum. We then sought the input of a young adult seminary graduate, who helped us refine and shape it. Then Gregg gave suggestions and developed the wisdom practices to be done between meetings. By the time the curriculum was finished, we all felt confident that something special would happen in these wisdom-mentoring groups.

Each of the sessions had a similar format. First, we started with a brief devotional thought from a particular passage of Scripture.

Next, we posed a challenging life situation, one that might be common for young adults. For example:

> Your friend has been diagnosed with a serious form of cancer that will require difficult treatment with an unknown outcome. You want to remain hopeful and encouraging to your friend, but inwardly you are worried and sad. Your friend mentions that the cancer has been difficult for her faith. She wonders how a loving and powerful God could allow such a thing. You've been pondering this too, and aren't sure how to respond to your friend's questions about faith.

After some brief group discussion, the group entered into a time of meditation and reflection. They pondered other scriptures, sat in silence, respectfully listened to God and one another, and didn't rush to fix the problem. Then the participants discussed what they learned about wisdom as they considered this difficult life situation alongside scriptures and group discussion. The final question each week went something like this: "How does today's conversation help you in relation to other life situations you are facing?" They were then assigned several wisdom practices to complete before the next group meeting.

One of the most important parts was selecting wise mentors. Gregg handled this task—and did so masterfully. The women and men he selected as wisdom mentors were gentle, godly, peace-filled followers of Jesus. Paul and I met with them several times for training, planning, and debriefing, and each time I felt enriched in their presence.

So far this sounds just like ministry, but remember the purpose was to marry science and ministry, so we did what social scientists do: we found a comparison group, selected a series of measures to administer before and after the wisdom-mentoring program, and then interviewed participants several weeks after the conclusion of the groups to get their impressions.

Our comparison group consisted of undergraduate students of approximately the same age living in the same community where the wisdom mentoring occurred. This worked fairly well because most of the wisdom-group members were also university students. We gave a number of self-report scales at the beginning and end of the study and also asked the mentors for some reflection on each of the group members.

The mentoring program lasted for twelve weeks, with six meetings on an every-other-week basis. Ideally, we would have had longer for this mentoring—it's hard to envision much growth in wisdom occurring over six meetings. Still, we found some intriguing differences between the wisdom group and the comparison group.

We observed an overall increase in life satisfaction among the wisdom group, but not among the comparison group (see figure 1.1).[9] This may mean that wisdom mentoring increases life satisfaction, or it could be that any sort of small-group meeting over twelve weeks is likely to increase one's satisfaction with life. But still, there is something particular about the group that promoted

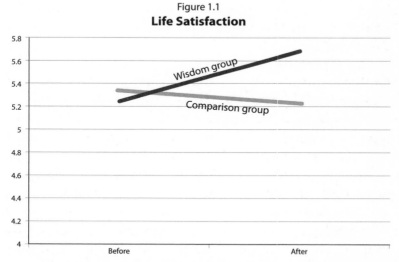

Figure 1.1
Life Satisfaction

Satisfaction with life was measured with the Satisfaction with Life Scale—5. The graph shows a significant interaction effect, with participants in the wisdom group increasing more than those in the comparison group. See Ed Diener et al., "The Satisfaction with Life Scale," *Journal of Personality Assessment* 49 (1985): 71–75.

wisdom. Note that scores for wisdom on the Practical Wisdom Subscale of the Wise Thinking and Acting Questionnaire increased for the wisdom-mentoring group over time, but not for the comparison group (figure 1.2).[10]

Those in the wisdom group reported more daily spiritual awareness than those in the comparison group, both before and after the wisdom mentoring occurred (figure 1.3).[11] Also, the wisdom group showed a statistical trend toward increasing more than the comparison group in daily spiritual experiences.

Perhaps the most important finding relates to a construct called "postformal thought." This is the ability to think about complex issues in flexible ways. Rather than coming to simple, rule-bound conclusions, postformal thought requires nuance and understanding of situational complexity. The critical wisdom of Jesus, discussed earlier, is an excellent example of postformal thinking. Similarly, the example of a fourteen-year-old girl who wants to

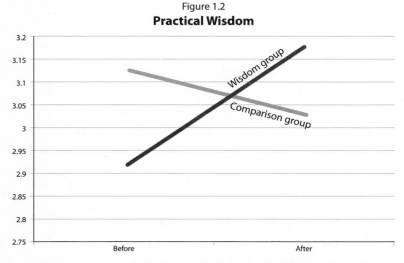

Figure 1.2
Practical Wisdom

Practical wisdom was measured with the Practical Wisdom Subscale of the Wise Thinking and Acting Questionnaire. The graph shows a significant interaction effect, with participants in the wisdom group increasing more than those in the comparison group. For details, see Katherine J. Bangen, Thomas W. Meeks, and Dilip V. Jeste, "Defining and Assessing Wisdom: A Review of the Literature," *American Journal of Geriatric Psychiatry* 21 (2013): 1254–66.

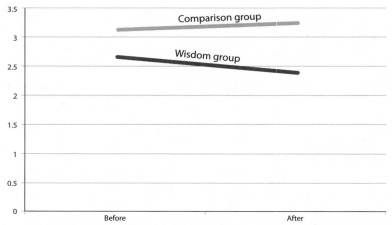

Daily spiritual experiences were measured with the Daily Spiritual Experiences Scale. Lower scores reflect more awareness of spiritual experiences. The wisdom group reported more spiritual experiences than the comparison group both before and after the wisdom cohorts, and the wisdom group also showed a trend toward increasing more in spiritual experiences than those in the comparison group. See Lynn G. Underwood and Jeanne A. Teresi, "The Daily Spiritual Experience Scale: Development, Theoretical Description, Reliability, Exploratory Factor Analysis, and Preliminary Construct Validity Using Health-Related Data," *Annals of Behavioral Medicine* 24 (2002): 22–33.

get married (see sidebar 1.1, on page 19) calls for complex post-formal thinking rather than an immediate and reflexive "No!" Two of the three subscales on our postformal thought measure showed meaningful changes over the course of wisdom mentoring (see figure 1.4).[12] These young adults learned to think in more complex, nuanced ways.

We also interviewed participants several weeks after the conclusion of the wisdom mentoring. Many participants spoke of how they learned to confront the complexity of life situations as they grew in wisdom. They emphasized their opportunities to observe wisdom in their mentors and practice it in their groups. One young woman put it this way:

What I really like about our wisdom study is that we didn't just sit down and try to hash out, here's a definition of what wisdom is.

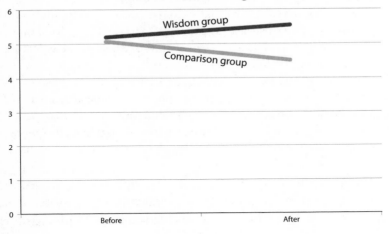

Figure 1.4
Postformal Thinking

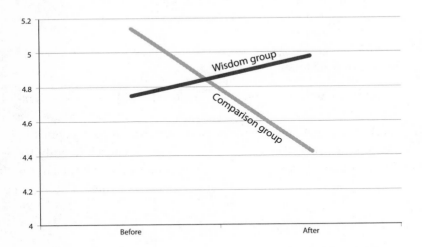

The top graph displays the ability to see underlying complexity in life situations. The bottom graph displays the ability to recognize that multiple "logics" may be applicable in a complex problem. Both were measured with the Complex Postformal Thought Questionnaire. The wisdom group reported increases as compared to declines in the comparison group. See Kelly B. Cartwright et al., "Reliability and Validity of the Complex Postformal Thought Questionnaire: Assessing Adults' Cognitive Development," *Journal of Adult Development* 16 (2009): 183–89.

It was more like . . . experiencing it. . . . Being a part of the group was experiencing it, because I think one thing I learned about wisdom is that it's something that's acquired through really studying God's Word and also hearing people. . . . So I think it's sort of that combination of what God's Word shows and also the Holy Spirit working and how he can work in other believers. So I think that was kind of what I came away with, was I just felt really encouraged by hearing . . . other people's perspectives and realizing that wisdom . . . doesn't have to be this overwhelming [thing]. . . . It was more like getting a chance to sit down and contemplate and have good conversations that I thought really helped me understand more.

As a social scientist, I was encouraged by this study in all sorts of ways, and it makes me want to study wisdom more in the years ahead. As a Christian, I was blessed by it deeply. Wisdom mentoring in the church works, and we can show at least some of its effects through scientific inquiry. This partnership between science and the church is exactly the sort of work that promotes meaningful dialogue about virtue in today's society.

Redeeming Wisdom

As outlined in the introduction, the purpose of this book is to redeem virtue in four ways: by helping Christians understand positive psychology, by seeing how Christian thought can change positive psychology for the better, by encouraging the church to embrace the science of positive psychology, and by considering implications for Christian counseling. Let's consider each of these.

Learning from Positive Psychology

I am fascinated by the science of wisdom, and I hope this chapter may generate curiosity among others as well. One of the reasons I find it interesting as an educator is that the task of education has changed drastically over my career. We used to emphasize knowledge, and now we teach wisdom. Or at least we try to.

When I studied for my doctoral degree at Vanderbilt University in the 1980s, I spent hundreds of hours in the university library, reading and memorizing information so that I could pass my classes in psychology and biochemistry (I minored in biochemistry at the medical school while completing my doctoral work in the psychology department). Much of my time was spent inputting information into my cortex through rote memory, rehearsal, and studying for exams. A more current version of that same information is now accessible to students in ten seconds if they move their thumbs quickly enough on their iPhone keypads. Just for fun, I computed the amount of information in the Vanderbilt library when I studied there, and it turned out that all the information in an impressive university research library could now be fully contained on a hard drive that is available for $99 on Amazon.com.

I recently began a chapel talk on wisdom at LeTourneau University by showing the students a picture of verticillium wilt—a problem that Lisa and I had in our tomato patch a few years ago. I challenged them to get out their phones and see how long it might take to discover whether verticillium wilt is caused by bacteria, fungus, insects, or lack of water. If I were researching a question like this back in the 1980s, it would require me to take a picture, run the roll of film to my local pharmacy for processing, pick up the pictures a few days later, then spend the day in the library looking through reference books on plant diseases. If I were fortunate enough to find the picture and diagnose the disease, I could then find additional books to figure out what sort of problem it is and how it is best treated. Granted, LeTourneau students are smart, and many are studying engineering, but within thirty-two seconds the students properly diagnosed verticillium wilt as a fungus, texted their answer to an online polling site, and watched their responses displayed on the chapel screen. The goal of education today is not inputting lots of information into a brain, as it was in my day, but properly discerning what information is good and valuable and what is not. Today we are bombarded with information, but some statements are more credible than others. How do we know the difference? Education today is more about wisdom and less about knowledge. Yet wisdom is as old as human history. It's fascinating to sit at the intersection of the very old and the very new and see what we can learn.

I also find wisdom fascinating as a psychologist, perhaps because the science flatters me. In several studies coming out of Germany, wisdom seems to be quite high among psychologists. The researchers considered that this might be because psychologists run the studies and somehow introduce a bias into how wisdom is measured. But when they found a group of nonpsychologists, nominated by others as exemplars of wisdom, the psychologists still ended up doing as well as the wisdom exemplars.[13] I'm not sure what makes it so—perhaps sitting with people in the most complex life situations year after year—but for some reason people in my profession appear to be quite wise. That makes me curious. Why would such a thing be? And to what extent are we drawing on the wisdom of counselors and psychologists in our church communities?

What Can Christian Thought Offer the Study of Wisdom?

In addition to finding the science of wisdom intriguing, I also find it frustrating. When positive psychologists started studying virtues a couple decades ago, they went to the religion and spirituality literature to identify the virtues and character strengths, and yet most social scientists have simply ignored what the major world religions have to teach us about those same virtues.

The scientific work on wisdom is helpful and fascinating, but the most revolutionary idea about wisdom that I have encountered is the theological distinction between conventional and critical wisdom. This distinction became the core of our church-based wisdom-mentoring program. More accurately, Jesus—history's greatest exemplar of critical wisdom—became the focal point for these groups. In Jesus we see one who shows incredible kindness and warmth to the disadvantaged even as he expresses outrage

at the injustices of calcified religion. In what may be the pivotal
verse of the Bible, John describes Jesus as full of truth and grace
(John 1:14). He is incredibly loving, forgiving, and merciful, and
he stands firm against injustice, treachery, greed, and oppression.
Being like Jesus, embodying critical wisdom, is our telos.

The Church Can Benefit from the Science of Wisdom

Perhaps the most exciting part of Paul's dissertation is that it
served the church well. Young adults learned from wisdom mentors, and they became more like Jesus in the process. The church
also modeled the sort of rich dialogue with science that helps
keep faith communities relevant in an age when science is revered,
probably too much.

At the final meeting with our wisdom mentors one of the questions that blessed me most was one put to us by a cohort leader,
who also happened to be the administrative pastor: Were they
free, the leader asked, to continue using the curriculum now that
the study was done? What a blessing to see this open partnership
between science and the church, one that leads to scholarly articles and books at the same time as contributing to the health of
young Christian adults. Everyone wins. Everyone strains toward
growing in wisdom.

Wisdom in Christian Counseling

Though we didn't consider the mentoring groups in Paul's study
to be counseling, it occurs to me that counseling clients come for
help because they are facing the same sort of quandaries in life
that we posed to our mentoring groups. People come for help
because they face difficult circumstances and want a companion
to join them through the dark valley. They come seeking wisdom,
embodied in the person of the counselor.

We dispense a good deal of conventional wisdom in counseling,
and in Christian counseling this is shaped by Christian thought.
In most counseling paradigms this is not done by the counselor

teaching or directly informing the client, but more by guided exploration as the client explores her or his feelings, beliefs, assumptions, behaviors, and priorities. Consider how the counselor is guiding the client toward conventional wisdom in the following hypothetical scenario.

CLIENT: I'm drowning in anxiety about all this. All she tells me is that she doesn't know if she loves me anymore, but I want to know what that means for our future. Is she leaving or is she staying? And every time I ask, she just turns and walks away, as if I've brought up some taboo topic.

COUNSELOR: And then when she walks away, your anxiety just goes wild.

CLIENT: That's exactly right. I mean, don't I have a right to know? Eighteen years ago my wife stood before God and two hundred people and promised me she would stay forever. What did that even mean to her?

COUNSELOR: [Pause.] And you're feeling all the weight of that, that sense that she promised something to God, to your friends and family, and to you, and now she may default on that promise.

CLIENT: [Long pause; tears of sadness.]

COUNSELOR: You talk about your anxiety, but I also hear a lot of emotion directed toward your wife. [Here the counselor is trying to help the client see his other emotions, besides anxiety for the future.]

CLIENT: What gives her the right to do this?

COUNSELOR: That's a big question, and an important one. When you ask that, "What gives her the right to do this?" what do you notice in yourself? [The counselor is turning the focus back to the client.]

CLIENT: It's terrible. I just get all tied up in knots. I can't think or do my job well or even sustain a meaningful conversation. It just overwhelms me. I feel this overwhelming urge to text her or call her and just force her to tell me what's going to happen. It's like she has all the control, and I have none.

COUNSELOR: I want to be sure I have this right. You have these feelings of anxiety and uncertainty about the future, then you start thinking these thoughts about the injustice of it all—what gives her the right? Then the feelings get almost out of control until you find a way to contact her. So you reach out to her, hoping for some reassurance.

CLIENT: Right. But I don't get any reassurance. Just more rejection.

COUNSELOR: So this isn't working very well for you.

The conventional wisdom here is related to what counselors call the pursuer-distancer dynamic in troubled relationships. As one person feels increasingly insecure, the tendency is to pursue the other. But in this case the client's wife already feels smothered, so she chooses to distance herself further from her husband, the pursuer. On and on the cycle goes, and both partners feel increasingly distressed and troubled. Offering the client insight into this cycle can be helpful in adjusting the relationship dynamics, and if his spouse is motivated to participate in counseling, it can be especially beneficial to have both partners aware of the cycle.

There is also a place for critical wisdom in Christian counseling—helping the client think outside the box and try something entirely different. Notice how he avoids his own anxiety by pursuing his spouse more actively. Not only does this not work but it also ends up exacerbating the anxiety he was trying to avoid in the first place. Avoidance strategies in general tend to add to the problem people are trying to avoid. Critical wisdom calls us to a different way of being, a new paradigm, even if the idea of such a thing seems outrageous at first.

COUNSELOR: So this isn't working very well for you.

CLIENT: No, it's really not.

COUNSELOR: Let me be audacious here. It's pretty clear how you want your wife to be—you want her to love you, to honor her commitments to you and to God, but let's go in a different direction for a moment. This is a defining moment in your life. Who do you want to be?

CLIENT: Huh? I don't know what you mean.

COUNSELOR: Just stand back and observe for a moment. There's a couple: the wife doesn't know what she wants, and the husband is terrified of losing her. How do you want him to act? Who do you want him to be?

CLIENT: [Pause.] Loving.

COUNSELOR: Say more.

CLIENT: I want him to stand by his wife, even if she refuses to do that for him. I want him to honor his promise to God even if she doesn't. I want him to find hope and maybe even forgiveness someday.

COUNSELOR: And as you say that, I see a calmer expression on your face, as if the anxiety monster steps back a bit when you focus on the person you want to be, the person you are becoming.

CLIENT: Yes, it does. I like how you put that, and it feels good to have the monster go away for a while.

If conventional wisdom helps the client see the pursuer-distancer dynamic in his marriage, critical wisdom helps him step outside to try something radically different. Pursuing his spouse is mostly a way to avoid anxiety, but it ends up adding to anxiety. In contrast, imagining the virtuous person he wants to be, the person he is becoming, has a calming and centering effect on him.

Life is filled with so many complexities, ranging from the trivial, such as playing football too long at an advanced age, to the tragic, such as the dissolution of a marriage or struggling with a life-threatening illness. In all the complexities we yearn for the virtue of wisdom to find our way forward, to find God amidst the silence of uncertainty, and to press toward becoming the full, flourishing, person God calls us to be.

2

Forgiveness

Forgiveness is close to the center of everything Christian. It shows up in the heart of the Lord's Prayer, which is in the middle of the Sermon on the Mount, which is the centerpiece of how we understand Jesus and his astonishing critical wisdom. "Forgive us our sins, as we have forgiven those who sin against us" (Matt. 6:12).

These words seep deeply into my soul. In a day when both the word and the concept of sin are quite out of style, I still ask God for forgiveness, believing that I am a sinner in desperate need of God's grace. Like centuries of saints who have gone before, I often pray a prayer so simple, yet profound, that it has become known as the Jesus Prayer. "Lord, Jesus Christ, Son of God, have mercy on me, a sinner." I sometimes shorten it and match it to my breathing: "God [inhale], have mercy [exhale]."

God, have mercy. Forgiveness, mercy, grace—these are what make Christianity Christian.

You may ask, what about love? Well, yes, love is the center of everything Christian too, along with faith and hope. But love flourishes only in the presence of forgiveness. Ask a happy young couple what lies at the heart of their success and you're likely to hear about love, at least if they are a young couple in a contemporary society influenced by Western thought. And they would be right. Ask a happy old couple the same question, and they will also say love, but will add that enduring love is possible only when alloyed with forgiveness, mercy, and grace. Hope also coexists with forgiveness. Imagine how dreary life might look if every emotional and interpersonal wound remained as fresh as the day it occurred. Cumulative bitterness. Hope emerges amidst the possibility that people and relationships can be restored from even the most painful lesions. And faith presumes this is so with God too.

The Science of Forgiveness

If forgiveness is at the center of Christianity, it has not been anywhere close to the center of social science, at least not until the past couple of decades.

In recent talks I have shown the graph in figure 2.1 to audiences and asked whether they could guess the label that belongs on

Figure 2.1
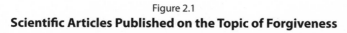

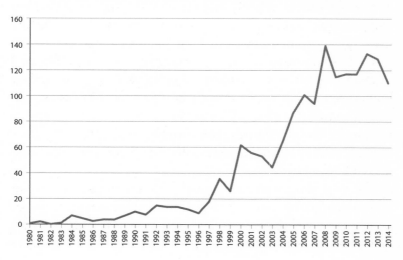

the y-axis. Most audiences are stymied, though a friend jokingly guessed it to be the price of Apple stock. It's not. The graph shows the number of scientific articles published on the topic of forgiveness over the past several decades. Back in 1980, as I was heading to graduate school and being warned of the evils of psychology by Christians, and the evils of religion by psychology students, no one was publishing about—or even studying—forgiveness. Back then it was common for psychotherapists to dismiss the possibility of forgiveness, arguing that it minimizes the pain experienced by past wrongs. Many psychologists ignored the topic, while others demonized it. Slowly, things started changing. Remember, it was 1998 when positive psychology was emphasized by the then–APA president, Martin Seligman. Around the same time the Templeton Foundation began funding various projects on forgiveness. Since then the topic has exploded. Research on forgiveness permeates social science journals and has found its way into bookstores, primetime television, and yes, psychotherapists' offices.

Imagine yourself as a counselor or psychotherapist working with Janice (a fictional client), a forty-two-year-old Christian woman who has suffered long because of childhood sexual abuse. Not only did her stepfather abuse Janice in her early teenage years but also somehow her mother failed to notice it. When she finally learned of the abuse, and her husband denied it, her first response was not to believe Janice. These wounds go deep and often turn an innocent life into a complicated mess. Somehow Janice has been able to build a career and a family of her own, but the memories still haunt her. How would you help Janice to heal from this tragedy? If you mention forgiveness too early, it might cause her to say the proper Christian words about forgiveness, but in a way that is shallow and superficial. If you give her ample room to explore her pain and never get around to the topic of forgiveness, you may be withholding her greatest hope of healing. Properly done, forgiveness can be an important part of counseling. We'll explore the mechanics of this later, but for now it's important to note that if Janice can successfully forgive her mother and stepfather, she is likely to lower her blood pressure, have less back pain, experience less muscle tension, and maybe even jump a little higher than she could before.

It turns out that forgiveness is good for us. As soon as the science of forgiveness started churning around the turn of the twenty-first century, we began seeing studies showing how various health markers correlate with forgiveness. Charlotte Witvliet and her colleagues published a groundbreaking study in 2001 after having seventy-one participants recall an interpersonal offense and then alternatively imagine an unforgiving or a forgiving response. Throughout the study participants were connected to psychophysiology-monitoring equipment, tracking their muscle tension, skin conductance (a measure of stress), heart rate, and blood pressure. As respondents imagined an unforgiving, grudge-holding response, the researchers found corresponding increases in all four physiological measurements. As the respondents moved into forgiving thoughts, their bodies became calmer again.[1] It didn't take long for this study to get noticed. Almost 30 percent of American adults have hypertension, and three-quarters of those take medication for their symptoms. What if forgiveness could provide another pathway to lower high blood pressure?

More studies followed. Kathleen Lawler and her colleagues at the University of Tennessee[2] monitored 108 participants with psychophysiology equipment as they were interviewed regarding hurtful experiences in the past. Those who reported being generally more forgiving people (i.e., trait of forgiveness) showed lower blood pressure than others. Those who reported more forgiveness for the particular event they described (i.e., state forgiveness) showed lower blood pressure, heart rate, muscle tension, and skin conductance than others. Again, forgiveness was linked to health markers that can have profound implications for heart health.

Even if you don't have hypertension, the chances are good that you will have lower-back pain. Between 60 and 80 percent of US adults experience lower back pain at some time in their lives. In 2005, James Carson and his colleagues studied back pain, anger, psychological distress, and forgiveness among patients from the Pain and Palliative Care Clinic at Duke University Medical Center as well as adults responding to newspaper advertisements in the surrounding area. The more forgiving among their group also reported lower levels of pain, anger, and psychological distress. Through correlational data—data from which one cannot infer cause and effect—the researchers observed that the connections between forgiveness, pain, and psychological distress appear to be mediated by anger, which suggests that reducing anger through forgiveness may also help reduce pain and distress.[3]

Also in the first decade of the century, Everett Worthington— a committed Christian scholar who is now one of the world's leading experts on the scientific study of forgiveness—made an important distinction between decisional and emotional forgiveness. *Decisional forgiveness* can occur quickly. It's when we decide to do our best to treat the offender the way we treated, or would have treated, the person before the offense occurred. This decision sometimes leads to *emotional forgiveness*, which occurs when our emotions, thoughts, and motivations toward the offender shift from a desire for retribution to wishing the person well. Emotional forgiveness may require months or years of work to be fully accomplished. Worthington and his colleagues published a helpful literature review in 2007 showing the various links between emotional forgiveness and health.[4] More than forgiving a particular offense (i.e., state forgiveness), being a forgiving person (i.e., the trait of forgiveness) seems especially important when considering health benefits. Put the other way around, those who are chronically unforgiving and angry are susceptible to a number of stress-related problems. Worthington and others also discussed the emerging evidence from medical trials showing that forgiveness interventions helped reduce risk in patients with heart disease and decreased relapse rates among patients with substance abuse problems; the scholars also highlighted some preliminary studies considering forgiveness among cancer patients.

SIDEBAR 2.1
Brief Forgiveness Glossary

As a scientist who studies forgiveness, I throw around some terms in this chapter that need explanation. Here is a brief glossary that may help.

Decisional Forgiveness

You have *decided* to forgive the other, though it is still a work in progress. If you find yourself bitter because a friend has never offered to pay you back the money that she owes, then you could decide to forgive your friend. This happens in a moment in time, though the fullness of forgiveness may not be so instantaneous.

Emotional Forgiveness

This happens when you have released the emotions of bitterness and anger and you wish the best for the one who has offended you. With your friend who owes you money, you have released feelings of ill will and forgiven the emotional debt, and perhaps also the financial debt. Emotional forgiveness is sometimes a long process.

Over the past decade, research has continued to emerge showing that forgiveness—especially trait forgiveness, sometimes called forgivingness—is linked to positive health markers. Compared to others, forgiving people have lower blood pressure and faster blood pressure recovery after feeling angry,[5] though the benefits of forgiveness go beyond just dissipation of anger.[6] When one person in a couple acts forgivingly toward the other, it lowers blood pressure for both the one wounded and the offender.[7] Cumulative stress is associated with poorer physical and mental health, but among those who are forgiving people, the link between stress and mental health problems is weaker than it is among unforgiving people.[8] Remarkably, people who experience the lightness of forgiveness perceive hills to be less steep and are even able to jump higher than those who continue to carry the burden of unforgiveness.[9] We also now have ample evidence that forgiveness interventions in psychotherapy are effective in

State Forgiveness

This is what you are experiencing at a particular time in response to a particular situation. On Monday you may feel complete release from bitterness toward your friend who is not paying you back, but then on Wednesday you might have a slight relapse and feel some unforgiveness. On Friday, you could be back to a place of full emotional forgiveness. When scientists measure state forgiveness, they always have a person imagine a particular situation and then have the person rate his or her current level of forgiveness.

Trait Forgiveness

This is also called forgivingness because it is a person's general disposition toward being forgiving. Some people find it easier to forgive than others, and so it is considered a personality trait. A forgiving person will have an easier time with decisional and emotional forgiveness of the person who fails to pay back money than a person who is low on forgivingness.

promoting forgiveness, reducing depression and anxiety, and increasing hope.[10]

Moving toward a Christian View of Forgiveness

Before exploring more of the science of forgiveness, let's consider two questions that may be troubling you, as they do me. First, with all the scientific evidence of forgiveness making us healthy, is forgiveness a self-help strategy? Should we forgive because it is a way to move on and become healthier, rather than allowing our offenders to continually rob us of our well-being? Seeing forgiveness as self-help may not be intrinsically wrong, but neither is it fully consistent with a Christian understanding of forgiveness. Second, there seems to be substantial imbalance in the forgiveness universe. We all seem quite fascinated with the science as long as we are forgiving those other people who hurt us, but why aren't we as interested in seeking forgiveness from those we have hurt? With so many who are wounded, and so few offenders, one has to wonder how the equation balances. Christianity can help us with both questions.

Beyond Self-Help

I once heard a pastor, who is also a theologian, describe Romans 15:7 as the second most important verse of the Bible: "Therefore, accept each other just as Christ has accepted you so that God will be given glory." Only John 3:16 was more important in the pastor's estimation. That sermon was twenty years ago, but it has lingered in my mind all these years. What would the world look like if we all accepted one another the way Christ accepts us? How might that affect our families, workplaces, churches, and communities?

So why do we forgive others when they hurt us? Is it because it helps us to move on with our lives, lower our blood pressure, and gain a stronger hope for the future? Well, yes. But as important as those outcomes are, the Christian is called to more. We forgive because of how deeply we have been forgiven. "If we reduce forgiveness to pop therapy, we ignore its invitation into the life that really is life."[11]

If Janice is to forgive her mother and stepfather for past events, she could focus on the personal benefits forgiveness will bring her, and it would be legitimate to do so. As a Christian, she could also work to immerse herself in a deeper understanding of the love of Jesus. Recall the apostle Paul of the New Testament, a man who experienced all sorts of offenses, including receiving thirty-nine lashes at least five times, being beaten with rods three times, and being stoned as a heretic (see 2 Cor. 11:24). This is the same man who taught that we should accept one another as Christ accepts us. Paul poses a sort of riddle in his New Testament letter to Ephesus: "And I pray that you, being rooted and established in love, may have power, together with all the Lord's holy people, to grasp how wide and long and high and deep is the love of Christ, and to know this love that surpasses knowledge—that you may be filled to the measure of all the fullness of God" (Eph. 3:17–19 NIV).

Did you find the riddle? Paul invites his readers to understand something we can never understand. God's love is too big to fully comprehend, and yet Paul prays that we might come closer and closer to grasping the love of Jesus. Sometimes as I'm pounding landscaping stakes into the hard ground, I flash to what it must have been like to be driving stakes through the hands and feet of God incarnate, and I get a glimpse of this love that is too big to fully see, love that chooses to hang on a cross despite excruciating agony and proclaims, "Father, forgive them, for they don't know what they are doing" (Luke 23:34).

Janice might experience lower blood pressure and a slight gain in vertical leap if she forgives those who have hurt her. Even more, she might have the opportunity to experience something of the fullness of Jesus.

Jeremy Taylor, a seventeenth-century Church of England minister, urged, "Call to mind every day some one of your foulest sins, or the most shameful of your disgraces, or your most indiscreet act, or anything that most troubled you, and apply it to the present swelling of your spirit, and it may help allay it."[12] Most of us probably don't do this every day, but if we did, I wonder whether it might help us to reflect on how deeply Jesus has forgiven us of our sins. Instead, our contemporary impulse is to reflect every day on how wonderful and talented we are. I wonder whether this contributes to underestimating or overlooking the depth of forgiveness that has been granted each of us.

Why do we forgive those who have hurt us? Because Jesus has forgiven us beyond what we could ever hope or imagine. Like a person reveling in an abundant fountain bursting forth on a parched summer day, so we are washed clean day after day by the lavish grace of God, which offers forgiveness for our wayward and selfish state as well as for the specific iniquities that taint our histories.

Ideally, Christian forgiveness is the exemplar of self-offering love, motivated by Jesus, who forgives out of immense love for us and at great personal cost. Jesus showed us how to forgive.

Imbalance in the Forgiveness Universe

If others are hurting everyone, where are all the hurters? Or might our self-perception be biased, so that we observe and remember when others hurt us and tend to minimize and overlook the ways we hurt others?

A Christian view reminds us that we are first forgiven, and second forgivers. Sometimes I fear the first half of this is lost on most of us, perhaps especially those immersed in today's popular portrayals of forgiveness. We see ourselves as forgivers more naturally than we see ourselves as sinners in desperate need of forgiveness from God and others.

I just mentioned the apostle Paul and all the forgiving he had to do because of the actions of his oppressors, but remember he was first an oppressor. Before his conversion on the way to Damascus, Paul was greatly feared by Christians because of how terribly he persecuted them. All of us have similar stories, though perhaps less dramatic, in which we give and receive harm. Somehow it's easier for most of us to remember the harm we have received than the harm we have given others.

Among the scientific articles reflected in figure 2.1, I would estimate that 99 percent of them pertain to forgiving others. A few scholars have studied seeking forgiveness, but these are not the studies that end up on CNN or the Huffington Post. When I speak on the topic of forgiveness, I find the same thing. People are fascinated with the idea of forgiving others. They eagerly ask questions and share stories. When we discuss being forgiven, the room goes silent.

We'll consider this more later, but for now let's hold the tentative possibility that (1) we tend to minimize our culpability in the problems of the world, and (2) we are a society of individualists. Rather than thinking about communities, and how we contribute to both the beauty and tragedy of those communities, we tend to see ourselves as individuals who are self-contained and self-determining. In this milieu forgiveness becomes more about me and the benefits I can gain than a reflection of my network of relationships in a larger collective. This is likely a consequence of science as well as the larger social Zeitgeist, and it reminds us how much we need the long historical witness of the church.

Forgiveness's Telos

Recall from the introduction and previous chapter that virtue is difficult for us to comprehend today because we have largely lost an understanding of teleology.[13] To understand any virtue, including forgiveness, we need to imagine how the fullness of that virtue would look in a person, and how regular people like you and I can move toward the goal of being whole and complete.

The first theological impulse with teleology, and the correct one, is to look to Jesus, the only fully functioning person ever to walk among us. With forgiveness, that appears to be a challenge because we can only see half the picture with Jesus. Yes, Jesus is the premier forgiver of all time. In him we see forgiveness in its human and divine fullness. Jesus "purchased our freedom and forgave our sins" (Col. 1:14). But what about the other half of forgiveness—seeking it when we have done a wrong to someone else? Christians believe that Jesus did no wrong, so never was in a position to confess and seek forgiveness.

If forgiveness is a virtue unto itself, then we have a problem viewing Jesus, who never needed forgiveness, as our exemplar. But if we expand our understanding of forgiveness to include a dimension of reconciliation, then we see the fullness of every virtue in Jesus, including the virtue of forgiveness.

Hold on to this thought for a moment as I describe a conversation I had with a focus group of five doctoral students, all young Christian adults studying to become clinical psychologists. They did not perceive themselves to be experts in forgiveness, though they were interested in the topic. I asked various questions about forgiveness, the church, and clinical practice, and what surprised me the most was how much they kept coming back to forgiveness and reconciliation. This is complicated because psychologists have historically wanted to separate the two. According to most psychologists I know, one can forgive without ever considering reconciliation. For example, imagine the abused spouse who lands in the hospital for the third time at the hands of a domineering and hostile husband. We might imagine that the abuse survivor could eventually forgive her husband, but it would be foolish for her to go back into that situation where she would likely be abused again. Seeing situations like this over and over throughout a career inclines psychologists to distinguish between forgiveness and reconciliation. Also, if reconciliation is part of forgiveness, then how can one forgive an offender who is already dead or who wants no part of reconciliation? There are good reasons psychologists distinguish between forgiveness and reconciliation, but this distinction was not so evident among the doctoral students in my focus group. One man pointed out that yearning for reconciliation might even be one of the reasons why people forgive. A young woman in the group agreed, noting how much she longed to make things right when she was at odds with another person. This is not to say that all relationships can be reconciled—as evidenced by the abused spouse in the hospital for the third time—but still, there may be some deep yearning for reconciliation that is, and should be, a part of forgiveness.

When Nathan Frise and I surveyed psychologists and theologians a few years back, we discovered that theologians are more inclined than psychologists to see reconciliation as part of forgiveness.[14] Theologians tend to view reconciliation, when it is possible, as the fullness of forgiveness, perhaps because they are more likely to think of telos than we psychologists are.

So now return to Jesus, who, though he never needed to seek forgiveness for doing wrong to another, spared nothing for the sake of reconciliation.

> When we were utterly helpless, Christ came at just the right time and died for us sinners. Now, most people would not be willing to

die for an upright person, though someone might perhaps be willing to die for a person who is especially good. But God showed his
great love for us by sending Christ to die for us while we were still
sinners. And since we have been made right in God's sight by the
blood of Christ, he will certainly save us from God's condemnation.
For since our friendship with God was restored by the death of
his Son while we were still his enemies, we will certainly be saved
through the life of his Son. So now we can rejoice in our wonderful new relationship with God because our Lord Jesus Christ has
made us friends of God. (Rom. 5:6–11)

It was Jesus who showed up on the shore after his resurrection
to cook breakfast for some of his disciples and have a healing conversation with Peter, the man who had denied him three times a few
days prior (John 21). Jesus taught in the most famous sermon of
all time that if someone has something against us, we should leave
our offering at the temple and go reconcile first (Matt. 5:23–24).
This Jesus, faultless and pure, the great forgiver, valued reconciliation above determining who is at fault for the rift.

> For God in all his fullness
> 	was pleased to live in Christ,
> and through him God reconciled
> 	everything to himself.
> He made peace with everything in heaven and on earth
> 	by means of Christ's blood on the cross.

This includes you who were once far away from God. You were his
enemies, separated from him by your evil thoughts and actions. Yet
now he has reconciled you to himself through the death of Christ
in his physical body. As a result, he has brought you into his own
presence, and you are holy and blameless as you stand before him
without a single fault. (Col. 1:19–22)

I should probably mention that Frise and I have taken some
criticism in the psychological community for our views that full
forgiveness may involve some degree of reconciliation when such

a thing is feasible, or at least a yearning for it. Our critics are among the leaders of the forgiveness movement in psychology, and people we have utmost respect for. Jichan Kim and Robert Enright responded with an article titled "Why Reconciliation Is Not a Component of Forgiveness,"[15] where they make an important distinction between human and divine forgiveness. They may well be right that our human forms of forgiveness are utterly different from how God forgives us, but it still seems to me that it is helpful to have a telos in mind. Jesus inspires me to yearn for reconciliation with both those I have hurt and those who have hurt me.

Scientific and Christian Forgiveness, Side by Side

Most Christians will agree that offering forgiveness is the right thing to do. We aspire to forgive, as God forgives us. But how do we do it? The practical day-to-day journey of forgiveness is arduous and taxing. Fortunately, we find help from those who have studied the psychology and theology of forgiveness.

Allow me to introduce you to three impressive forgiveness scholars, all of whom have my profound respect. One is a psychologist (and a friend), Everett Worthington Jr., a professor at Virginia Commonwealth University and the former mentor to many of the Christian psychologists studying positive psychology whom I will cite throughout this book. I mentioned Worthington earlier in this chapter because of his scientific work on forgiveness and also noted that he has become one of the world's foremost experts on the topic. His expertise is demonstrated by his many books, grants, studies, and scientific articles on forgiveness, and because his seventy-six-year-old mother was sexually violated and brutally murdered on New Year's Day 1996. Worthington's brother, who was the one to find his dead mother, committed suicide five years later. This personal journey of forgiveness has involved Everett forgiving his mother's killer and also forgiving himself for not being able to help his brother.[16]

The second is a theologian, L. Gregory Jones, who is executive vice president and provost of Baylor University. Jones has written many books, including *Embodying Forgiveness*[17] and *Forgiving as We've Been Forgiven*.[18] He offers great theological wisdom to the study of forgiveness while also being a social critic of how psychotherapists have diluted the construct, reducing it to a pallid, therapeutic shadow of what God intends. In *Forgiving as We've Been Forgiven*, Jones teams up with coauthor Célestin Musekura, a Rwandan scholar and pastor who experienced incredible loss as a result of the genocide in Rwanda. In 1997, three years after establishing African Leadership and Reconciliation Ministries (ALARM), Musekura lost five family members and seventy members of his church in revenge killings that were aftershocks of the genocide. His commitment to forgiveness has been costly—including accusations that he is a traitor to fellow Hutus, beatings, and being held in a government torture room for several hours.[19]

These three—Worthington, Jones, and Musekura—have important perspectives for us to consider when it comes to how we forgive. Because one is a psychologist and the other two serve in theology and Christian ministry, considering their perspectives allows us to put psychology and Christianity side by side. Specifically, let's consider the step-by-step models of forgiveness they propose and how they compare and contrast.

Honest Exploration of Pain

All three experts agree on how to start the forgiveness journey. In his REACH model, Worthington[20] talks about the importance of recalling the hurt. We can't forgive someone by simply ignoring or condoning or disregarding the offense. When we have been hurt, we need to honestly acknowledge it, lean into the pain, feel it deeply, and become familiar with its texture and contours. Our lives are sometimes changed by the hurts we receive, and it does us further harm to deny the damage that has been caused.

SIDEBAR 2.2
Worthington's REACH Model of Forgiveness

Worthington's REACH model has been tested in various scientific studies and found to be a helpful and effective way to forgive.*

Step 1. Recall the Hurt

Be honest about the harm done. It's not helpful to deny the pain or the hurt. Accept it and be honest about it.

Step 2. Empathize

This is tough, but try to understand what the other person might have been thinking and feeling. How would the other person describe what happened?

Step 3. Altruistic Gift

Forgiveness is ultimately a self-offering gift we are giving to the other. Instead of wishing the other person harm, we decide to wish the other well.

Step 4. Commit

Commit to forgiving the other. This may involve telling a pastor or counselor, a partner or a friend. *Whom* we tell isn't as important as *that* we make a commitment to forgive.

Step 5. Hold On

Forgiveness isn't easy. We may readily slip back into unforgiveness, making it important to have ways of holding on to our commitment to forgive.

*Everett L. Worthington, *Forgiving and Reconciling: Bridges to Wholeness and Hope* (Downers Grove, IL: InterVarsity, 2003).

If Janice wants to truly forgive her stepfather and mother, it will likely call her into the valley of the shadow of death, where she reflects deeply on the pain the abuse caused her. Sin has profound consequences, and Janice bears those consequences every day in how she understands sexuality and how she relates to people she wants to trust.

Jones and Musekura[21] speak of the "dance steps" of forgiveness, which is an appealing metaphor in that it reminds us that each individual step is just a part of a larger and more beautiful goal. We learn the steps in order to engage in the amazing dance of forgiveness. Their first two steps, like Worthington's first, involve an honest leaning into the hurt that has been done. Jones and Musekura describe this as speaking honestly and patiently about the conflicts (step 1), and then acknowledging the anger and bitterness we feel along with a desire to overcome these feelings (step 2).

I recently had lunch with a psychologist who claimed that he could help his clients reach full forgiveness in a single forty-five-minute session, regardless of how intense the offense against them might have been. While I respect this man's work, I disagree. This first part of the forgiveness process—telling the story, recalling the hurt, acknowledging the full brunt of anger and bitterness caused—can take many weeks or months, or even longer. Jones and Musekura put it simply: "Forgiveness takes time."[22]

Considering the Offender

This is tough. When we are hurt deeply, we tend to view the offender in monstrous terms. "He is nothing but a ____." "She is such a ____." We naturally fill in the blanks. But all people are more complex than the labels we use to describe them. Worthington's second step is experiencing empathy for the offender, and Jones and Musekura's third step is summoning concern for the other as a child of God.

Forgiveness requires us to move beyond simple categories and labels, and to see complexity in the person who hurt us. As Janice continues in the forgiveness process, she will need to consider what sort of unacceptable urges her stepfather may have been dealing with over many years. This is not to excuse what he did, but to try to understand the complications of his life. Similarly, Janice would do well to consider the situation her mother was in when

Jones and Musekura's "Dance Steps" of Forgiveness

Jones and Musekura offer the following six steps for forgiveness. They use the metaphor of dance steps, reminding us that we need to learn some steps before engaging in the beautiful dance of forgiveness.*

Dance Step 1. Truth Telling

Forgiveness requires that we speak the truth of what happened, even knowing that our view may differ from the perspectives of others. "We must . . . take the time to talk to one another about the things that divide us."† This is not easy and calls for both honesty and patience with one another.

Dance Step 2. Acknowledging Anger

To forgive, we must journey through an awareness of our anger and bitterness. Though hatred can be transformed to love, we first acknowledge the depth of our emotional pain in order for this transformation to occur.

Dance Step 3. Concern for the Other

As difficult as it sounds, forgiveness calls us to see the other as a child of God. Even if we hold the other person in utter disdain, God sees past the sin and loves the other person deeply.

she first learned of the abuse. Why might she have not believed Janice? Could it have anything to do with her mother's own longings for love and connection? Might she have used denial as a way to cope with the awful news she was hearing for the first time?

It is essential that understanding not be confused with condoning. It's not okay what Janice's stepfather did to her, and her mother's first reaction was still the wrong one, but as Janice develops greater understanding of the others involved, she will move forward on her forgiveness journey.

We psychologists tend to make forgiveness an individual and interpersonal endeavor, but Jones and Musekura put the forgiveness act squarely in the context of Christian community. We learn

Dance Step 4. Recognizing, Remembering, Repenting

Though it is important not to discount the power difference between offender and offended, it is also good to recognize that we naturally see the fault in others more quickly than we see our own. We may never have done the sort of thing our offender did to us, but we all are capable of hurting others and then cloaking our offense in denial and self-deception.

Dance Step 5. Commitment to Change

Forgiveness requires that we look forward, not just backward. This will involve personal change, as we move away from bitterness and toward wishing the best for the other. It also involves community change as we strive toward greater justice and wholeness.

Dance Step 6. Hope for the Future

Even if reconciliation is not possible, we move forward to a place where we recognize our yearning for reconciliation. This involves a yearning for reconciliation with our individual offender as well as a larger awareness of how deeply we need reconciliation amidst our faith communities.

*L. Gregory Jones and Célestin Musekura, *Forgiving as We've Been Forgiven: Community Practices for Making Peace* (Downers Grove, IL: InterVarsity, 2010).
†Ibid., 47.

the dance steps of forgiveness not so we can dance alone in the living room, but so we can dance with others in celebration of our good and gracious God. And Christian community turns out to be a great way to better understand the other, including those who have offended and hurt us.

A Christian understanding of sin, experienced relationally, is helpful in promoting empathy and concern for the other. In Christian community, sin is not just a list of bad things people do, or good things they fail to do, but rather the fallen state in which we live both individually and collectively. Our perceptions, beliefs, actions, and feelings fall short of the full human experience that God intended us to have. We limp as crooked people and broken communities through the years of our lives, falling short in various ways, and this applies to every one of us. As we forgive, we can remember that though we may never imagine ourselves doing what our offenders may have done to us, each of us has wounded others in various ways. We are both the offended and the offender. This is the fourth dance step in Jones and Musekura's model, that we recognize our complicity in the problems of the world and the problems in our own communities and families.

Committing to Forgiveness

After exploring the pain and working to understand the other, forgiveness ultimately comes down to a commitment. We decide to forgive, or not to forgive.

Janice has now walked through the valley of the shadow of death. She has wept and shuddered in anguish. She has considered what her stepfather and mother might have been experiencing all those years ago, and what they may have experienced since. Now she faces a decision. Does she hold on to the bitterness, or does she release it and choose to forgive?

Worthington's third step is offering the altruistic gift of forgiveness to the offender. Rather than choosing bitterness, the forgiver chooses to wish the other person well. The fourth step is to make a commitment by talking to a friend, partner, counselor, or pastor about the decision to forgive. This resolution to forgive isn't going to be easy, so committing to another person is an important part of the process. The fifth step is holding on to the decision. Even after one decides to forgive, the emotional fullness of that decision may take many months or years to accomplish, and Janice may be tempted to go back on her decision to forgive many times. Forgiveness requires the tenacity of holding on.

Similarly, Jones and Musekura emphasize the commitment required to forgive. Their fifth step is committing to struggle through the change process. While psychologists tend to emphasize the emotional and relational work this requires, Jones and Musekura also talk about striving for justice. Forgiveness often involves efforts to make things right with a community.

Yearning for Reconciliation

At this point we see a departure between Worthington's model and the model proposed by Jones and Musekura, and between a psychological view of forgiveness and a theological one. In the REACH model, holding on to forgiveness is the final step, and a clear distinction is made between forgiveness and reconciliation. According to Jones and Musekura, there is one more step to consider, and that is the yearning for reconciliation. Though reconciliation may or may not ever happen, they believe a full process of forgiveness at least calls us to yearn for reconciliation. Janice may not be able to reconcile with her stepfather after all these years. Maybe he is dead, or long vanished from Janice's life, or perhaps her stepfather is unwilling to have a conversation with Janice. But still, she wishes that she could somehow have a healed and safe relationship with the man who hurt her so much. Reconciliation, or at least yearning for it, is the telos of forgiveness.

Redeeming Forgiveness

Let's work to redeem forgiveness using the same four strategies we'll use for each of the virtues considered in this book: learning from positive psychology, seeing what Christian thought can offer, considering how the science of forgiveness can help the church, and pondering how Christian counseling might embrace this virtue.

Learning from Positive Psychology

Perhaps it is wise to start with two questions, and then we'll add a third later. The first question is, why should we forgive? Positive psychology has helpful information to offer, as outlined at the beginning of this chapter. Forgiving promotes health in the forgiver. Do you want lower blood pressure, less back pain, less anger, less anxiety, more hope? Forgiveness is likely to help.

Second, how do we forgive? Do you sit in a church service convinced that you want to forgive the person across the room who hurt you two years ago, or twenty, but unsure how to go about doing it? Again, positive psychology provides helpful answers. Worthington's REACH model has been tested repeatedly, and it works. People can learn to forgive and can experience the many benefits associated with forgiveness.

What Can Christian Thought Offer to Forgiveness?

The same two questions should be considered again, but from the perspective of what the church can offer to the science of forgiveness, at least for those who are part of a community of faith. Why should we forgive? Yes, there are plenty of ways forgiveness promotes individual health, but it also promotes community health. Both in a sole-authored book[23] and in his book with Célestin Musekura, L. Gregory Jones speaks wisely to the community benefits of forgiveness and to the dangers of relying too much on the individual therapeutic benefits of forgiveness. We forgive because we have been forgiven, because the church is to mirror the truth and grace of Jesus. In this place of community it is difficult to draw the clean lines between forgiveness and reconciliation that psychologists have often drawn.

How do we forgive? The church hasn't always been clear or helpful in this regard, but let's not forget how Christian teaching can help us forgive. Strangely, though there is now a large psychological literature on forgiveness and a surprisingly large literature on prayer, almost no one in the scientific community has considered how prayer and forgiveness go together. (Everett Worthington is an exception in his remarkable book *Forgiving and Reconciling*.) Yet this has been the essence of the church's teaching for centuries. When some students and I asked one hundred Christians to describe how they forgave a significant offense, half of them mentioned prayer without us even telling them what we were looking for in the study.[24] We were looking for prayer. Later, a dissertation student and I looked at how a prayer intervention promotes forgiveness, and we found that it enhances empathy for the offender.[25] This is not news for those steeped in Christian thought.

The Church Can Benefit from the Science of Forgiveness

Once we've considered why and how we forgive, the third question to consider is where we forgive. Those who have been Christians for any significant amount of time recognize how challenging it can be to remain in fellowship with one another—all of us sinners attempting to become better at emulating the grace of Jesus.

A church is a vulnerable place where we learn about one another's foibles and weaknesses and vulnerabilities. And in the process we hurt one another with alarming frequency.

I've often imagined what a body might look like if healing were impossible. Just picture every blemish, abrasion, scab, and wound you have ever experienced all being present in your body right now. It's not a pretty picture. How handicapped and impaired and ugly would the body of Christ, the church, be if forgiveness were not possible?

Where do we forgive? We forgive in lots of places, but perhaps especially inside the community of faith, where we have ample opportunities to wound one another and also to learn about and grow toward the character of Jesus. If the science of positive psychology can help us even a little bit with the mechanics of forgiveness, then the church stands to become a more beautiful reflection of God's presence in this broken world.

Forgiveness in Christian Counseling

I make the case in the introduction that there aren't many good bridges between positive psychology and counseling, and while that is true for most virtues considered in this book, it is not true for forgiveness.

Nathaniel Wade, whom I first met when he was an undergraduate at Wheaton College, where I was teaching at the time, recently published a meta-analysis of all the published and unpublished studies he and his colleagues could find on psychotherapeutic interventions for forgiveness.[26] After graduating from Wheaton, Wade went on to get a doctoral degree at Virginia Commonwealth University, where he studied with Worthington. Wade, Worthington, and two other colleagues found fifty-four studies looking at forgiveness in psychotherapy, and sure enough, forgiveness interventions help people to forgive. Forgiveness interventions also help people become less depressed and anxious and become more hopeful.

Christian counselors would do well to become familiar with the work of Worthington and also the pioneering work of Robert Enright,[27] both of whom have written and done research on clinical applications of forgiveness. Their work is exemplary and evidence based. Importantly, both Enright and Worthington attend to the long, arduous process involved. Forgiveness takes time, and it is important to allow the wounded person ample time to explore the pain that was caused. Otherwise forgiveness becomes something more like excusing or condoning, but not true forgiveness.

Given that chapter 1 advocates a sort of critical wisdom that invites us to think outside the box, let me suggest three outside-the-box sorts of ideas for Christian counselors. First, most clients will be motivated by the personal gains that forgiveness offers. It helps them move on with their lives, and that is a good thing. Christian counselors can both celebrate this motive, because it is a good one, and remember that other motives are important also. The Christian idea of forgiving as we have been forgiven not only promotes forgiveness of an offender but also deepens faith and awareness of God's profound gift to us. So yes, let's consider the personal benefits of forgiveness with our clients, but at least with Christian clients we do not need to stop there. Considering other reasons to forgive may promote growth in various virtues, including the Christian virtues of faith, hope, and love.

Second, though it is not feasible for every forgiver to reconcile with every offender, neither is it essential to shut off conversations about reconciliation in counseling. The person who has been assaulted over and over by a partner would not be wise to reconcile and go back into the relationship, but that does not mean that some yearnings for reconciliation will never show up. As forgiveness progresses, it is quite likely the wounded soul will express some longing for a family to be made whole again, even though it seems impossible for such a thing to happen. The sensitive counselor remains wise, likely reminding the client of how this just can't work given the past record of behavior, but still validating the yearning. This is the telos of forgiveness, to yearn for reconciliation, whether or not it can ever happen. The same is true for a forgiver whose offender is dead. Reconciling can never happen this side of eternity, but the forgiver can yearn for it. And this is a sign of fullness and virtue when it happens.

Finally, we Christian counselors need to remember the other half of the forgiveness equation. Sometimes people come not seeking to forgive as much as seeking forgiveness. Self-forgiveness, which I explore briefly in chapter 6 under the heading "Science and Grace, Side by Side," is part of this, but so is seeking forgiveness from the person the client has hurt. We need ears to hear this. Too often we assume that clients come to us because they have been deeply wounded by others, and that is often true, but sometimes they come because they have been the offender and are looking for a way to move forward in life.

In all these ways, we can seek to keep Christ in the center of Christian counseling. Jesus is the benchmark of virtue, the one who shows us the way when we are confused and self-deceived.

Forgiveness is close to the center of everything Christian, and Jesus, the great forgiver, is the exemplar of our faith. May we have eyes to see and ears to hear Jesus in our churches, our counseling offices, and even in our science.

3

....

Gratitude

What's wrong? As in right now, at this moment in your life, what challenges and struggles do you face in life? Perhaps a meaningful friendship is strained, or someone you care about is ill, or you are facing a serious illness. Maybe money is tight, or the obligations of life are suffocating you. Perhaps you are in a committed relationship and longing to get out, or not in a committed relationship and longing to get into one. Are you facing habits or addictions that exert more power in your life than you want, or is someone you love in trouble? Maybe you're concerned about a child, grown or otherwise. Problems with anxiety and depression may be nipping at your heels. There are so many troubles in life, and every day our mind gravitates toward them in various ways.

To give up thinking about the troubles in life is likely impossible. These are real problems, and they demand our attention. But this chapter attempts to call us to a place of balance.

What's right? Right now, at this moment, what are the gifts and blessings that envelop you? If you're outdoors, you might pause and notice cloud formations in the sky, remembering that the clouds will never be in exactly the same configuration again.

Notice the sounds around you, the smiles on the faces of people you meet, the gifts of good food, air to breathe, and the beauty of the present moment. Perhaps you think of people—those you have known in the past, and those you know today. These are people who have gifted you with presence, with wisdom, and perhaps with love. Consider the privilege of knowing how to read, of living in a time with the convenience of indoor plumbing, electricity, and smartphones. Ponder the gifts that God gives—the gift of grace and life and hope, the life-changing gift of Jesus. Think of the people who believe in you, those who inspire you, those who have been kind and understanding and warmhearted. Allow yourself to consider and appreciate all these gifts, to settle into a space of gratitude.

The previous paragraph uses the word "gift" seven times. My choice of connecting gratitude with gifts is not coincidental, because the two are related. "*Gratitude* is a sense of thankfulness and joy in response to receiving a gift, whether the gift be a tangible benefit from a specific other or a moment of peaceful bliss evoked by natural beauty."[1] Most of us have had the experience of giving a gift to an ungrateful receiver. "This is not the right color." Or, "Oh, I was hoping for [fill in the blank]." Or, "Where's my next gift?" And likely we've had the opposite experience, a joyous one, where the one receiving our gift wells up in tears of thankfulness. This is the difference between entitlement and gratitude, and it turns out to be a distinction of great importance to our physical, emotional, and spiritual well-being. May we learn to be the one who thankfully receives the gifts offered to us every day. May we well up with gratitude toward God and one another.

Luke tells a quick story about gratitude, sandwiched between stories of faith and apocalypse in chapter 17 of his Gospel. Jesus heals ten lepers, and one—a cultural outsider—returns to acknowledge the profound gift of healing he has received. Each of us has the opportunity to be the one who chooses gratitude amidst the struggles of life.

Is Gratitude a Virtue?

Look at the classic Hellenic virtues—prudence, justice, fortitude, and temperance—and gratitude is nowhere to be found. Add in the Christian virtues—faith, hope, and love—and still, gratitude doesn't make the list. Consider the seven heavenly virtues that stand in contrast to the seven deadly sins—chastity, temperance, charity, diligence, patience, kindness, and humility. Still, no gratitude. So is gratitude even a virtue, and if not, what is it doing in a book titled *The Science of Virtue*?

This conversation goes back to Aristotle, one of the Greek philosophers who shaped how we have considered virtue for the past twenty-three centuries. Aristotle saw virtue in conferring benefits to the other. The virtuous person is a giver, not a taker.[2] In one regard, this view has great appeal. If society were composed of those who saw virtue in receiving gifts more than giving them, just imagine the problems we would have with entitlement and passivity. According to the apostle Paul (Acts 20:35), even Jesus taught, "It is more blessed to give than to receive."

Still, I think we should consider gratitude a virtue. First, Aristotle was writing in a pre-Christian context. Virtue to Aristotle was seen in the strength of giving to others, and this is certainly consistent with the character of Jesus, who devoted himself to compassionate care for those around him. But the culmination of Christ's life, death, and resurrection, unknown to Aristotle, turns giving and receiving upside down. The essence of Christ-following is that we receive before we give. We are those whose strength is discovered most fully amidst our weakness (2 Cor. 12:10), those who confess we are not sufficient to save ourselves. We are the healed lepers, and hopefully we are the one in ten who returns to give thanks for the gifts given us by Jesus. In fairness to Aristotle, it should be noted that some contemporary philosophers think there may be more room for gratitude in an Aristotelian view of virtue than previously thought.[3] It is also worth noting that Cicero—a Roman philosopher writing a couple centuries after

Aristotle, and one whose writings later influenced Augustine toward Christianity—described gratitude as the "parent of all virtues."

Second, in the introduction to this book I make the case that virtue causes us to get our eyes off ourselves and onto the other. Christian virtue is seen most fully in loving God and neighbor. In this regard, gratitude is a virtue because it moves us beyond our natural inclination for self-focus and allows us to see—and be thankful for—the other. Psychologist Robert Emmons identifies our excessive sense of self-importance as the greatest obstacle to a life of gratitude, and so it has always been.[4] Gratitude calls us toward humility, recognizing that we cannot and need not be self-sufficient.

Third, I appeal to common sense about a life well lived. Years ago our friend Mike posed this question to Lisa and me as the three of us were enjoying a meal together: "When you're eighty years old, sitting on a rocking chair on the front porch, what will really matter to you then?" I've reflected often throughout my life on Mike's question, perhaps all the more so as I move decade by decade closer to eighty. When I think about living, aging, and dying well, my mind goes to gratitude. I doubt I will sit on my porch at eighty and think, "I gave more than I received." I hope I won't just think of my regrets, though I'm sure I will do that some. Instead, I hope to ponder the many gifts that life has offered. Some are offered over many years, such as the love of a companion, and some are fleeting, such as the birdsong on a particular summer morning or the taste of a fresh Oregon strawberry. To whatever extent I have discovered grace in my life, I suspect my mind will rest quietly on this greatest gift of all. I already sense it happening, and I trust it will continue if I am blessed enough to live until, or beyond, age eighty. And if I do, I hope to spend quite a lot of time on the rocking chair on the front porch pondering Mike's question and all that has passed in the intervening years.

Huston Smith, a renowned expert in philosophy and world religions, wrote what may be his final book at age ninety-three, *And Live Rejoicing.*[5] The final section heading in his book is titled "The Two Categorical, Unconditional Virtues," referring to gratitude and empathy. The two are highly related, as grateful people tend also to be empathetic.

In Luke 18, Jesus tells of two men praying in the temple. One, a Pharisee, had a shallow form of gratitude devoid of empathy: "I thank you, God, that I am not like other people—cheaters, sinners, adulterers. I'm certainly not like that tax collector! I fast twice a week, and I give you a tenth of my income" (vv. 11–12). The other, a "despised tax collector" (v. 10), offered simple words that have been reverberating throughout all Christianity for two millennia: "O God, be merciful to me, for I am a sinner" (v. 13). Known simply as the Jesus Prayer, these words reflect a posture of humility, embedded in the virtues of gratitude, as the pray-er anticipates the gifts of forgiveness and grace, and of empathy, as the pray-er refuses to elevate self above other and sees the sameness that extends through all humanity.

The Science of Gratitude

Not many scientific studies change the world, but the scientific world was nudged substantially in 2003 when two Christian scholars, Robert Emmons and Michael McCullough, published findings of three randomized gratitude trials in a major scientific journal. In one of their studies, they randomly assigned undergraduate students to one of three conditions. One-third of the students were told to keep a gratitude journal each week. A second group made a list of the hassles they faced that week. A third group, which served as a control, simply described some events of the week. The students did this for ten weeks; then the researchers followed up with them for nine additional weeks. Those in the hassles group looked about the same as those in the events group by the end of the study, but those in the gratitude group responded in some interesting ways. It wasn't so surprising that gratitude journaling increased optimism, favorable life ratings, and so on. But Emmons and McCullough also found that those randomly assigned

SIDEBAR 3.1
Gratitude Journaling

It's likely you have heard of gratitude journaling by now, but not too many years ago it was a new idea. Robert Emmons pioneered the use of journaling in his many studies on gratitude and has summarized many of the most important findings in *Gratitude Works!**

Here are the instructions that Emmons and McCullough used in their landmark study on gratitude journaling:

There are many things in our lives, both large and small, that we might be grateful about. Think back over the past week and write down on the lines below up to five things in your life that you are grateful or thankful for.†

The basic idea is to write about several things you have experienced recently for which you are grateful. Write a sentence about each. Emmons provides some other keys to successful gratitude journaling in *Gratitude Works!*

1. Don't overdo it

It turns out that journaling every day may not be as effective in promoting gratitude as doing it a couple times a week. Emmons calls this phenomenon "gratitude fatigue."

2. It's okay to remember problems and struggles

We may tend to think gratitude requires pushing problems out of consciousness, but this is not the case. Recalling a past failure or struggle

to gratitude journaling reported exercising more, sleeping better, and visiting the doctor less often than those assigned other forms of journaling. Emmons and McCullough then conducted a similar study with a group of patients with neuromuscular diseases, using daily gratitude journals rather than weekly, for twenty-one days. Again, they found those in the gratitude condition to report more positive emotion, less negative emotion, and more optimism. The gratitude group also reported being more connected with others, sleeping more than those in the control group, and feeling more refreshed in the morning. In interpreting these results, it is often primes us to consider breakthrough moments, or to anticipate them, and in the process to encounter gratitude and hope.

3. Subtract

"Count your blessings" sounds like an addition equation, but try subtracting as you journal. Imagine what life might be like without your child, partner, faith, job, or community. This helps us to recognize the gifts in life we might easily take for granted.

4. Surprise!

Look for surprises in life, as they engender more gratitude than most routine events.

5. People over things

It's fine to be grateful for a new boat or an old house, but even better to be thankful for the people in your life, past and present.

For more on gratitude journaling, see Emmons, *Gratitude Works!*, or check out Jason Marsh, "Tips for Keeping a Gratitude Journal," Greater Good Science Center, November 17, 2011, http://greatergood.berkeley.edu/article/item/tips_for_keeping_a_gratitude_journal.

*Robert Emmons, *Gratitude Works! A 21-Day Program for Creating Emotional Prosperity* (San Francisco: Jossey-Bass, 2013).
†Robert A. Emmons and Michael E. McCullough, "Counting Blessings versus Burdens: Experimental Studies of Gratitude and Subjective Well-Being," *Journal of Personality and Social Psychology* 84 (2003): 379.

important to note that these studies used experimental designs with true random assignments. That is, participants in the study did not self-select as to which experimental condition they would participate in, but were selected randomly and then assigned to a particular experimental condition. This is the gold standard in social science research, meaning that we can infer some level of causation.

In other words, gratitude changes us. Near the end of their scholarly paper, Emmons and McCullough report about an upward spiral, where gratitude makes us more prosocial and more attuned to our social networks and how these networks bring love and belonging. The researchers also note that gratitude promotes spiritual awareness, broadens emotional and cognitive flexibility, and helps us resist stress.[6]

Interest in gratitude was beginning when Emmons and Mc-Cullough published their findings, but since that time it has exploded. In the past fifteen years, dozens of additional studies have linked gratitude with mental, physical, and spiritual health. I'll not attempt to review the entire gratitude literature here, but will highlight a few key findings.

Gratitude Is Good for Your Health

If you spend much time on the internet or reading popular magazines, you've probably seen quizzes and checklists about how to live a healthy life. Don't smoke, drink a little alcohol but not too much, eat plenty of fruits and vegetables and not too much saturated fat and sugar, watch your weight, wear your seat belt, avoid unsafe sex, exercise 150 minutes per week, and so on. It's striking how rarely these lists include psychosocial factors, such as gratitude. There is now a large body of research evidence demonstrating the connection between gratitude and health.

Alex Wood of the University of Manchester and his colleagues published a helpful review in 2010 showing the numerous connections between gratitude and psychosocial health.[7] Gratitude is associated with increases in positive mood, pleasantness, self-esteem, sense of well-being, and life satisfaction. Grateful people have a lower risk of depression than others, as well as a decreased likelihood for anxiety disorders, phobias, eating disorders, nicotine dependence, and alcohol/drug abuse. Grateful people are less materialistic than others and experience enhanced daily motivation.

Wood and his colleagues go on to summarize how gratitude promotes social relationships. Compared with others, grateful people are more motivated to work on their relationships, more inclined to repay kind gestures, and more willing to forgive. They are inclined to praise and trust others, to accept altruistic acts from

others, to help others, and to feel socially supported. Those who
are grateful tend to have positive views of others, to be expressive
of their feelings, and to find meaningful ways of resolving conflict.
Though most of the studies reported by Wood and colleagues
are correlational, the evidence supports the likelihood of some
causal links between gratitude and wellness. Consistent with this,
evidence reported by Sara Algoe and her colleagues suggests that
expressing gratitude in a romantic relationship promotes improvements in the relationship over the coming six months.[8] Moreover,
gratitude from one partner promotes gratitude in the other.[9]

More recent evidence hints at connections between gratitude, spirituality, and cardiovascular function. Paul Mills and
colleagues[10] report that among heart failure patients gratitude
is associated with better sleep, less depression, less fatigue, and
improved biomarkers of inflammation. These same outcome variables are associated with spirituality, but the authors report that
the connection between spirituality and these health markers is
largely explained by the increased gratitude that spiritually inclined
people experience. In a follow-up response, Mills reports that
using gratitude journaling as a way to promote gratitude among
heart failure patients had physiological benefits. He and his colleagues conclude, "Gratitude journaling is a low-cost and easily
implementable intervention that may have significant beneficial
effects to enhance health in cardiac patients. A more grateful heart
may indeed be a more healthy heart."[11]

The focus on gratitude and heart health represents quite a shift
since the days of my graduate training. In the 1980s, those interested in behavioral medicine were considering the negative aspects
of emotions and how they affect heart health. Much was made of
the Type A personality—the person who felt constant pressure to
get more and more done in less and less time. Researchers deemed
this sort of high-pressured lifestyle to be related to negative heart
health. While this connection remains likely, researchers find so
many mystifying exceptions that identifying someone as Type A
or not isn't that helpful. Today's research in behavioral medicine

tends to consider more positive emotion, such as gratitude, and how it may be related to health.

What about Gratitude Interventions?

Because most studies on gratitude and health show that the two are positively correlated, I can assert with confidence that gratitude is good for health. The link between the two is strong and robust in the scientific findings: grateful people experience various psychosocial health benefits, relational benefits, and likely physical health benefits as well.

But can people who are not naturally grateful learn to become more grateful? And if they do become more grateful, will they experience the same health benefits as those who are naturally grateful? The evidence on this is not crystal clear.

Let's back up a minute. Earlier in the chapter I mentioned some landmark studies by Emmons and McCullough showing that gratitude journaling produced all sorts of good outcomes in college students and adults with neuromuscular disease. When published, these findings garnered a good deal of attention. It seemed clear that gratitude interventions make people healthier. Not surprisingly, gratitude exercises gained popularity. Smartphone apps were developed, popular books were published, and bloggers promoted gratitude journaling. But how effective are these exercises?

Scientists use something called an effect size to determine how powerful an intervention is. An effect size of 0.2 is considered relatively small, 0.5 is moderate, and 0.8 is large. When the gratitude-journaling group was compared with those who wrote about the hassles of life, the effect sizes for promoting gratitude in Emmons and McCullough's studies were 0.56 and 0.88. These are respectable effect sizes, but not all subsequent studies have shown equally strong effect sizes.

When multiple studies are conducted on a topic, it allows researchers to do a meta-analysis, where a number of published and unpublished studies on a topic are considered, as with the forgiveness meta-analysis described in chapter 2. Don Davis and his colleagues recently completed an extensive meta-analysis on gratitude interventions and discovered that the average effect size is about 0.46 when a gratitude exercise (e.g., gratitude journaling) is being compared to an alternative exercise (e.g., hassles journaling).[12] But one must question whether writing a hassles journal might actually add stress to a person's life, so a better comparison might be to look at gratitude journaling versus no intervention at all. When that is considered, the average effect size shrinks to 0.2.

The other question to ask is whether measuring gratitude is the best outcome measure for gratitude studies. Gratitude journaling may enhance gratitude, at least a little, but if we're claiming that gratitude has other health benefits, then the effect sizes for these other health markers may be more meaningful than simply measuring changes in gratitude. When looking at psychological well-being variables, Davis and his colleagues found that gratitude interventions outperformed no intervention at all (average effect size of 0.31) and showed very modest improvements over the alternative exercise, such as hassles journaling (average effect size of 0.17).

What do all these numbers mean? Gratitude interventions, such as journaling, may help a little if people want to be more grateful and psychologically well, but the effect sizes are not particularly impressive. Adding gratitude exercises to one's daily "to do" list will probably not be as helpful as other health behaviors. Buckle up. Eat more plants. Exercise. And yes, be grateful, but don't expect as many health benefits from this as you might from the others.

Here's a quick summary. It's compellingly clear that grateful people are healthier than others. It's not so clear that gratitude interventions make people more grateful. Some people are just naturally more grateful and will have health benefits because of it. Others have to work at becoming more grateful, and though the work will likely help their health and general levels of gratefulness, the amount of the benefit may not be large.

Moving toward a Christian View of Gratitude

My wife, Lisa, who has a PhD in sociology and has written a book on the topic of contentment,[13] has been a good conversation partner for me as I write this chapter. This morning, over oatmeal with fresh Oregon blueberries, I summarized the science of gratitude for Lisa, as I have just done in the preceding paragraphs. Her response took me aback, and rightly so.

After hearing the summary that some people are just naturally grateful and that efforts to increase gratitude are not always strikingly effective, she looked quizzically at me and questioned why this even matters. In her mind—and I think she is right about this—it's not particularly relevant whether we reap benefits for being grateful. Gratitude is simply the way we are called to live as Christians. It may be tougher for some people than others, and it may or may not make us healthier, but moving toward more and more gratitude in life is still part of our calling. It's who we are to be, regardless of how good it may be for our health.

In her latest book, *To the Table*, Lisa describes quite a lot about the agricultural lifestyle we now live and how it points us toward gratitude.[14] I'll illustrate this with a honey harvest example.

For most of a decade now we have been amateur beekeepers. Most years we have four colonies of Italian honeybees, though keeping hives alive through the winter has become increasingly difficult with the prevalence of colony collapse disorder. But on the good years—and we have some—we harvest honey in mid-August. "Harvest" is a bit of a euphemism because it really means we steal the honey the bees have worked all summer to accumulate. (In our defense, we leave them plenty for winter and steal the extra they have made.) Once we gather all the honey frames from the hives, we carry them up to our potting shed, where we set up a centrifuge and spin out the honey from the comb. We then transfer it to jars and save it for our own use or sell it to members of the community-supported agriculture farm we operate each summer.

Harvesting honey turns out to be messy business. It's sticky stuff, and we get a fair amount of it on our hands as we move the frames in and out of the centrifuge, and into the glass storage jars. This means we wash our hands many dozens of times on honey harvest day. As Lisa moves toward the sink in the potting shed, she often takes the opportunity to lick some honey off her fingers before washing her hands, and when she does she always offers a small expression of delight. Sometimes she'll say, "Oh my!" Sometimes it's just, "Mmmmmm." It's almost involuntary for her. Honey evokes delight, as it should. And this may be the best metaphor I can offer for gratitude and Christian living. In blogging about it, I summarized it this way: "Lisa's exuberant moan of delicious gladness was almost involuntary, as if gratitude requires sound effects. That's how I want to live, and not just in response to honey. I want to sigh in delight when I see the hills on the horizon or breathe the crisp air of an autumn morning, when I visit with my children and grandchildren, when I encounter a fresh idea, and when I reflect on the joy of good work."[15] Is gratitude good for our health? Maybe. But that's not really the main point of the Christian story, is it? Amidst the various struggles and challenges of life—and every life has them—we have been given the most incredible gift. It is the gift of abundant life in Jesus, and the most reasonable response is to give thanks.

I have included a number of gratitude practices in sidebar 3.2 that are consistent with a Christian life. They may or may not lower our blood pressures or add years to our lives, but they reflect the way we are called to live as Christians.

Gratitude's Telos

In each of these chapters we have been glimpsing the notion of telos—what a fully functioning person might be in relation to the virtues we are considering. As discussed, Aristotle saw the "great-souled" person to be a giver and not so much a receiver, but in a Christian worldview we are inevitable receivers.

Gratitude Practices

Here are some practical ways to practice gratitude.

Mixing Up Mealtime Prayers

Christians who use ad lib prayers before meals and those who use a standard prayer at mealtime may both find themselves in a similar place of saying habitual words that merely bounce off the ears rather than penetrate the soul. Maybe it's time to try something new.

Write a Psalm

A standard gratitude exercise is to write a letter to someone who has influenced you in a positive way. Some take this a step further and suggest you visit the person and read the letter aloud. These are great ideas, but here's a variant that might promote both gratitude and awareness of God. Try writing grateful words to God, perhaps in the form of a psalm. Write about God's faithfulness, goodness, and love, and how you have experienced it daily. As with King David in the Old Testament psalms, it's okay to express some questions and spiritual struggles also, but begin and end the psalm with affirmations of God's goodness. And if you're feeling bold, try reading it aloud when you are done.

I picture Jesus in the upper room just days prior to his crucifixion, offering to wash Peter's feet. At first Peter refuses, perhaps aligning himself with the great-souled person that Aristotle had envisioned several centuries earlier: "No," Peter protests, "you will never ever wash my feet!" Like Peter, I tend to be fiercely independent, earning my way, insisting that I am okay without the help of others.

Jesus says to Peter, and to me, "Unless I wash you, you won't belong to me." And here is the invitation that changes Peter's life, and mine, and changes that of anyone else who chooses for it to be so. We can stand on our own, insist on our sufficiency, be the great-souled individualists, or we can humble ourselves and recognize how profoundly we need what Jesus offers. Like the tax gatherer in the temple, we can simply respond, "O God, be

Prayer Stroll

Take a leisurely walk and notice the sights, smells, and sounds of your community. Notice the aroma of fresh pizza being baked, the brightness of the sunshine or freshness of the rain, the exuberance of children. Again, this is a standard gratitude activity, but try adding a prayer component to the stroll. Speak with God as you saunter along. Tell God what you notice, what you love about this good life. Thank God for the beautiful gifts to be experienced every day and for joining you on your stroll.

Daily Examen

A common Jesuit practice is the Daily Examen, a prayerful pause in the evening to reflect on God's presence throughout the day. The examen involves being aware of God's presence, remembering the day with gratitude, paying attention to your own experiences and feelings, choosing one part of your day for prayerful reflection, and looking ahead to tomorrow.

Journaling

Gratitude journaling has been used in many scientific studies of gratitude and has been linked with various positive health outcomes (see sidebar 3.1 for more information).

merciful to me, for I am a sinner" (Luke 18:13). Peter uses different words to express a similar idea: "Then wash my hands and head as well, Lord, not just my feet!" (John 13:9).

And so here is the telos of gratitude, summarized in three basic steps—not coincidentally the same steps identified by Christians who are doing research in gratitude.[16] First, we recognize a gift is being offered, however undeserving we may deem ourselves to be. Second, we recognize the source of the gift to be outside ourselves. Someone else is offering us this gift. Third, rather than resisting the gift and insisting on our own sufficiency, we gratefully receive it, acknowledging the goodness of the gift and the giver.

Social scientists call this benefit detection: having eyes to see the gifts given us, even in times of distress and trouble. Not surprisingly, it turns out that religious involvement and religious forms of coping can help promote benefit detection, and therefore gratitude.[17]

This is the simple rhythm of gratitude—humbly noticing the gift, seeing the giver, and receiving both. And when we engage in the rhythm, we invite the upward spiral that Emmons and McCullough describe so well: we invite meaningful relationships to develop, become more attuned to spirituality, become increasingly compassionate toward others, and learn to be kindhearted and flexible in how we view ourselves and those around us.[18] The upward spiral invites us to heightened awareness of the gifts present in everyday life, and in so doing invites us deeper into the spiritual life. The more grateful we are, the more grateful we become, and the more we see God's fingerprints on every gift life offers.

Scientific and Christian Gratitude, Side by Side

So again, as in every chapter, we ask how we should hold science and faith together, allowing both to enrich our understanding and conversations. Experientially, this seems quite a natural connection, especially in relation to faith communities. Lisa's sound effects while harvesting honey symbolize how I want to live life, being gratefully aware of all the gifts life offers and then living each day in celebration of these gifts. But in reality I easily allow myself to be hindered by the responsibilities and challenges facing me. I have too much to do most days, and often that clutters my vision for gratitude. And it turns out that I am a sinful person, prone to look at life through the filter of self-interest, which keeps me thinking of myself far too often at the expense of noticing the gracious gifts that life presents every moment. The grateful way I want to live is not the reality I experience every moment. I just wish there were a reset button, to bring me back to a centered way of living where I can breathe in the grace God offers me every moment and notice the many gifts that make life rich and meaningful.

Wait. There is a reset button.

Lisa and I attend services each Sunday morning at Newberg Friends Church, an evangelical Quaker gathering best known as the place where Richard Foster was pastor as he authored *Celebration of Discipline*. As we participate in this community of friends, joining together in singing, learning from the weekly sermon, finding opportunities to serve others in loving ways, listening to God in corporate silence, we find ourselves recentered and refocused, week after week. With spiritual centeredness comes greater awareness of virtues.

> Since God chose you to be the holy people he loves, you must clothe yourselves with tenderhearted mercy, kindness, humility, gentleness, and patience. Make allowance for each other's faults, and forgive anyone who offends you. Remember, the Lord forgave you, so you must forgive others. Above all, clothe yourselves with love, which binds us all together in perfect harmony. And let the peace that comes from Christ rule in your hearts. For as members of one body you are called to live in peace. And always be thankful. Let the message about Christ, in all its richness, fill your lives. Teach and counsel each other with all the wisdom he gives. Sing psalms and hymns and spiritual songs to God with thankful hearts. And whatever you do or say, do it as a representative of the Lord Jesus, giving thanks through him to God the Father. (Col. 3:12–17)

Gratitude and worship belong together. Surprisingly, the science of gratitude has not considered the role of faith communities until recently. Jens Uhder, one of my former doctoral students, completed his doctoral dissertation looking at gratitude campaigns in two local churches. Both Jens and I are grateful for the support of the John Templeton Foundation in funding his research.[19]

His study involved what is called a crossover design, depicted in figure 3.1. During the first four weeks of the study, the first congregation engaged in a special ministry focus on gratitude. This involved a sermon series, a small-group discussion of a book about gratitude, and encouragement to participate in various gratitude exercises,

Figure 3.1
The Crossover Design Used in Dr. Uhder's Dissertation

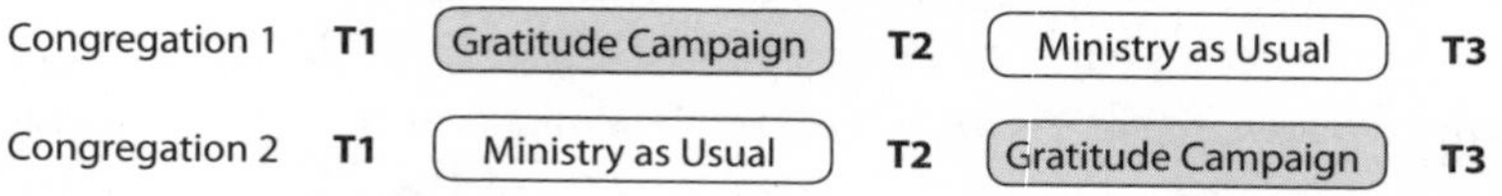

Congregation 1 **T1** [Gratitude Campaign] **T2** [Ministry as Usual] **T3**

Congregation 2 **T1** [Ministry as Usual] **T2** [Gratitude Campaign] **T3**

such as gratitude journaling, counting blessings, and writing about three good things in life. After four weeks, the first congregation went back to ministry as usual, and the second began the gratitude focus. We measured both congregations at three times—before the first congregation began the gratitude focus, at the crossover point, and at the conclusion of the study. The measurements included dispositional gratitude, positive and negative emotion, life satisfaction, psychological well-being, spiritual well-being, daily spiritual experiences, interpersonal engagement, and religious behavior.

Jens and I expected to find that Congregation 1 would show positive increases during the four-week gratitude emphasis and that similar changes would not be seen in Congregation 2 until after the crossover point. We were only half right. Indeed, Congregation 1 showed the expected changes during the first four weeks of the study—increases in satisfaction with life, psychological well-being, positive emotion (and decreased negative emotion), daily spiritual experiences, and attitudes toward psychology. Though we expected Congregation 2 to hold steady during this first four weeks of the study, because they were not yet engaged in their gratitude ministry, this did not happen. All the good changes that happened in Congregation 1 also seemed to happen in Congregation 2, even before they engaged in the gratitude ministry (see figures 3.2 and 3.3).

We are puzzled by the results. Perhaps just anticipating the gratitude ministry was enough for folks in Congregation 2 to become more grateful as Congregation 1 engaged in their gratitude campaign. Perhaps just regular ministry enhanced gratitude in Congregation 2 during the first four weeks of the study. It's also possible that simply answering the items on the various questionnaires primed people to become more grateful, regardless of

Figure 3.2
What We Expected

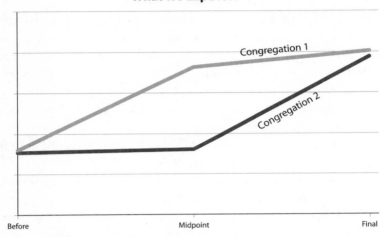

Figure 3.3
What We Found

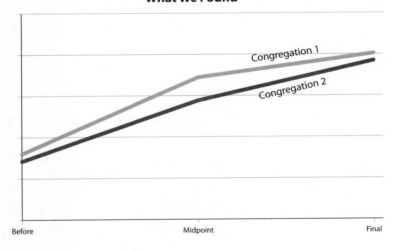

whether their congregation was engaging in the gratitude ministry over the coming four weeks. Or maybe the changes were related to extraneous factors, such as moving from the short, rainy days of an Oregon January into the more hopeful days of February.

But here's the most likely explanation. Our groups started out
too grateful and healthy to detect the sort of subtle changes we expected. Social scientists have a measure called skewness to describe
a distribution on a scale. As it turns out, almost every one of our
measures was seriously skewed in a direction known as a ceiling
effect. Even before the study began, people who responded to the
questionnaires reported being highly grateful, satisfied with life,
psychologically well, and spiritually attuned. Yes, they continued
to improve throughout the next four weeks, but with the ceiling
effects being so pronounced, we wouldn't expect to be able to
detect much nuance in the changes.

Clearly, more research is needed to understand gratitude in
faith communities, but here's what we know so far. Churchgoers,
at least those in Jens's study, were—by and large—already grateful and well adjusted. Special ministry campaigns may or may
not help promote gratitude. My hunch is that any sort of special
ministry emphasis is not nearly so important as ongoing church
involvement.

Redeeming Gratitude

Learning from Positive Psychology

The positive psychology of gratitude reflects a large body of
science that would be impossible to summarize in a few sentences.
But fools rush in, so let me give it a try. We know that grateful
people are relationally and emotionally healthier than others, and
probably physically healthier as well. It also seems clear that delib-
erate efforts to enhance gratitude help some, but not as strikingly
as might be alleged by the marketers of the latest gratitude app.

What Can Christian Thought Offer to Gratitude?

Christianity has much to offer to the science of gratitude. Much of
it goes back to that breakfast conversation with Lisa that I described
earlier. As a scientist I want to measure the effects of gratitude, but

as a Christian I ought to have motives for grateful living that are much bigger than what the immediate outcomes may be. Pursuing gratitude because it helps me sleep better or live longer or go to the doctor less often can become quite a self-centered endeavor. Paradoxically, a full-bodied gratitude calls us away from self-centeredness toward an empathetic ability to see the other, to pause in worshipful reflection as we recognize the many gifts offered to us.

Here are three other ways Christianity can contribute to the science of gratitude. First, many of the world's leading scientists studying gratitude are Christ followers. It's so encouraging to me as a psychologist to see the influential role that committed Christian scholars are making, such as Robert Emmons (cited frequently in this chapter and arguably the world's leading expert on the topic of gratitude). Second, the Christian faith has a historical and theological depth that is desperately needed in studying gratitude. Because we know gratitude works to promote all sorts of good things, many people are now interested in becoming more grateful. But grateful for what? And to whom? By offering answers to these questions, Christianity promotes a full-bodied gratitude among those who seek it. Third, Christianity can help us understand the virtues of Christian community and how such a community promotes gratitude. Something about giving and receiving care in the context of ongoing, faith-based community may promote all sorts of good outcomes, including gratitude. We need to keep studying this, of course, but it's interesting that our initial study didn't work out very well, in part because people in these faith communities were already so grateful and healthy that they didn't have much room to grow.

The Church Can Benefit from the Science of Gratitude

For better or worse, science reflects the ethos of the day. The church can ignore science, or even fight against it, but to do so is to risk cultural irrelevance, perhaps driving away those who seek to follow Jesus.

A better response is to understand and even embrace the science. It helps us to learn a good deal about the positive life of faith that we aspire to live. While it is true that science alone does not address the deep metaphysical realities that give meaning to the good life, it is still important to embed conversations about the good life into the prevailing paradigms of knowledge that are part of today's culture.

By learning something of the science of gratitude, we are reminded that one of the dimensions most central to Christianity—giving thanks to our good and gracious Creator—is good for us, for those we love, and for our communities.

Gratitude in Christian Counseling

Most of my comments to Christian counselors in this book are related to the counseling process, but in this chapter I offer a few comments to counselors themselves. Everyone who has done counseling for more than a few weeks recognizes that the work is arduous and demanding. The suffering of the world has a way of settling heavy on counselors, and before we know it we are easily bogged down with the pain all around us. I suspect the same is true for pastors, though I have never done that work.

This is the world that Jesus came into, to shine light in the darkness (John 1:4–9). We who bear witness to the light of Jesus are called to recognize the great gifts that God offers—the gifts of nature, of relationships, of grace and salvation, of hope and faith and love. Renewed by these gifts, we enter into the heavy lifting of counseling knowing that the good somehow outweighs the bad even when it is difficult to see how.

This renewal can be challenging, especially when the heaviness of suffering settles on us day after day, but this is part of the calling to the work of Christian counseling, and so it behooves us to find ways to practice gratitude. It may or may not help us live longer or have better blood pressures or enhance our overall life satisfaction, but it will reacquaint us with the light of Jesus in those times when darkness seems to be winning. The more we practice gratitude, the more it becomes automatic when we need it the most.

For me, church brings me back to gratitude week after week. So does working in the dirt, spending time with my family, singing praise choruses in the car, or just sitting silently as I drive and noticing the glorious world around. May we all find our way back to gratitude, back to the light of Christ, day after day after day.

4

Humility

In Christian circles we often think of humility as antipride. Pride, that great vice from which all other vices flow, has been widely recognized as a huge problem. C. S. Lewis describes pride as the "essential vice, the utmost evil," noting that "it is the complete anti-God state of mind."[1] Lewis points out that humility is the virtue in opposition to the vice of pride. While I concur with Lewis, it seems troublesome that we so often speak about humility based on what it is *not*, rather than what it *is*. Positive psychology makes an important contribution in this regard by articulating the nature of humility without contrasting it too much with pride. We'll get to definitions later, but for now it is enough to say that humility involves a reasonably accurate view of oneself, a concern for others, and an openness to various ideas.

Humility is a challenging topic precisely because the least humble people are likely to see themselves as the most virtuous, including the virtue of humility. Besides, most of us are apt to see our strengths more clearly than our weaknesses, so it's fair to say that almost everyone believes himself or herself to be more humble than the average person—something that is statistically impossible.

In preparing for this chapter, I have challenged myself to consider the obstacles I face in becoming humble. It's difficult work, because, like most people, I'm more inclined to see how I *am* humble rather than how I am *not* humble. Still, as I've pondered the matter, I find many obstacles in my quest for humility. Some I might categorize as the obvious suspects related to pride: I think about myself more than is necessary or reasonable; I struggle with arrogant attitudes, especially when I believe myself to be more informed or wise on a topic than another person; and often I assume the best when considering my own motives for saying or doing something and assume the worst when considering others' words and actions. (It might be worth noting that in this paragraph-long discourse on my struggles with humility the pronoun "I" shows up twelve times.)

But the most surprising challenges to humility have been the subtle influences that often sneak beneath my awareness because they are not matters of pride, character, or moral choice, at least not overtly so. Here are two examples. First, over the past decade I have experienced increasing hearing loss. For the first few years I was convinced that Lisa was not speaking clearly or loudly and told her so. (Okay, so there may be some pride involved with this part, but the greatest obstacle to humility is yet to come and not as closely tied to pride.) Then my students started speaking more quietly, and my friends too. Eventually I faced the truth and started wearing hearing aids, which has helped me to confront an obstacle to humility that was so subtle I hardly noticed.

For a number of years I have feigned understanding in many of my conversations with others, learning to smile and nod at strategic moments rather than risk saying something completely off-topic. I feign engagement outwardly, but inwardly I have retreated into my private world. Hearing became such hard work that even when I could hear, I often chose to take the easy path, pulling inward. Until I started hearing again, with the help of some amazing devices, I didn't realize how this affected my capacity for humility. If humility involves an ability to understand and care about the other, then my hearing loss became an obstacle to humility. Now I face the task of relearning how to engage with others, enter into their words and emotions, and care about them deeply. I don't assume that my struggle is necessarily true of others with hearing loss. I offer this as a personal example rather than any sort of general statement about how hearing affects humility.

The second place of conviction has been my busyness. We live in a time when being busy is respected, often admired, and I have let myself slip further and further into the vortex of what Richard Foster calls "muchness and manyness" as the years have passed.[2] Though I cannot deny that subtle pride drives some of my overcommitment, much of my busyness is also connected to good motives—trying to help students, colleagues, and family members with the skills and knowledge I can offer. Still, my humility suffers as a result. The busier I get, the more I spend my few spare moments thinking about myself—what I am falling behind on, what I need to do later today or tomorrow, how others are intruding on my time, what will happen to my reputation if I fail to follow through on a commitment, and on and on it goes. Busyness robs me of the freedom to rest in God and consider others as it propels me into a near obsession with my own obligations and commitments. At least for me, being overly busy is the antithesis of the great commandments—to love God and to love others as self. If I cannot think often and well of others, then I am not being humble. This problem is not so easily resolved as the first. I daresay it has become my greatest obstacle to humility, and one that I need to address courageously in the months and years ahead.

I offer these personal examples at the beginning of this chapter because I recognize my quest for humility, and my battle against self-centeredness, to be a common human experience. Others face different obstacles than I do, but we all experience barriers to humility. For some it may be success, for others failure. For some it is inflated self-esteem, for others it is a deflated view of self. For some it is exceptional health, for others it is sickness. Still, we press on toward humility, knowing it is the way Jesus would want us to live and the way he himself lived among us.

It's Absurd

Karl Barth, the great twentieth-century Swiss theologian, described "the absurd contrast." In all of human history there is only one person who has had the right to assert superiority over others, and what did he do? "He gave up his divine privileges; he took the humble position of a slave and was born as a human being. When he appeared in human form, he humbled himself in obedience to God and died a criminal's death on a cross" (Phil. 2:7–8). And the rest of us, what do we do? We so often scramble around trying to figure out who is better than who and how to win the contrived competitions of life to prove our worth. Barth was right. It is absurd.

David Brooks, author of *The Road to Character*, points out various ways we have become even more absurd in recent decades. In Brooks's compelling book he suggests that contemporary society is becoming increasingly like the chest-thumping NFL linebacker who has just made a good tackle. We have become nearly obsessed with self-promotion, following our hearts, trusting ourselves, and seeing ourselves as special. Brooks compares decades past to the current day:

> But it did occur to me that there was perhaps a strain of humility that was more common then than now, that there was a moral ecology, stretching back centuries but less prominent now, encouraging people to be more skeptical of their desires, more aware of their own weaknesses, more intent on combatting the flaws in their own natures and turning weakness into strength. People in this tradition, I thought, are less likely to feel that every thought, feeling, and achievement should be immediately shared with the world at large. . . . There were no message T-shirts back then, no exclamation points on the typewriter keyboards, no sympathy

ribbons for various diseases, no vanity license plates, no bumper stickers with personal or moral declarations. People didn't brag about their college affiliations or their vacation spots with little stickers on the rear windows of their cars. There was a strong social sanction against (as they would have put it) blowing your own trumpet, getting above yourself, being too big for your britches.[3]

Brooks's words remind me that in the past six weeks I have posted a political opinion, a drone image of our house with our newly installed solar panels, and a picture of our summer garden. In the meantime I have not posted on Facebook, nor have I ever, anything about how prone to selfishness I can be when my schedule gets overwhelmingly full, how I fret inanely about aging, how often I give in to eating sugary foods that are not good for me, how easily I assume foul motives in others when they disappoint me, or even if they just disagree with me. In short, I fuel my pride on Facebook, but never admit my pride.

Once a man lived on earth who had every right to blow his own trumpet, as Brooks would say. He lived without flaw, loved beyond belief, taught with powerful wisdom. Instead of promoting himself, he showed humanity the deepest sort of humility and love we have ever seen.

Humble at the Core, with an Arrogant Crust

How can we reclaim the virtue of humility amidst a cultural milieu of self-promotion? Surprisingly, I suggest that both science and the church can help. It turns out that both parties are intrinsically humble, yet it is sometimes hard to notice because they are composed of many individuals who are notoriously arrogant.

Science is intrinsically humble because of the scientific method, which assumes that people are easily self-deceived, with the result that actual observable data need to be collected and analyzed to serve as a check and balance for our natural errors in understanding the world. And even when the data are collected and analyzed, good science insists that findings be replicated to see whether conclusions are responsible. Rarely will a person find the word "proven" in a scientific journal. We evaluate, build theory, evaluate more, refine our theories, evaluate again, and on and on science goes, marching toward truth. Science is enforced humility, but all of us can think of scientists who shatter this picture with remarkable arrogance and overconfidence. In a time when scientific knowing is elevated—and sometimes assumed to be the only legitimate way to know a thing—it is easy for scientists to begin thinking of themselves as all-knowing.

Similarly, the church—the bride of Christ—is intrinsically humble because the church is built around Jesus, the one who humbled himself even to the point of death. The story of life is not so much our personal story, or a story about how we should be happy and fulfilled, as it is a story about a loving and just God who continually calls us to relationship. And if my life story is not primarily about me, then humility is the natural outcome. The more I touch the truth of God's purposes, and the more I get my eyes off myself and onto Jesus, the more I begin loving God with my whole being and my neighbor as myself (Matt. 22:37–40). Like science, theistic religion is intrinsically humble, but again, it doesn't take long for any of us to think of Christians who crush this image. Some of the greatest human atrocities in history have occurred in the name of Christianity. We hold zeal, truth, commitment, and faithfulness as important values, and they are, but sometimes we hold them so tightly that we slip into places of incredible arrogance.

This conversation between science and the church will succeed only if we can reclaim humility in ourselves and in our dialogue with one another. As is true in any relationship, the conversation breaks down if we perceive one party to be humble and the other to be arrogant. As a member of both parties in this conversation, I suggest that we scientists and we Christians are called to be humble. Yet we fight our arrogance too, because our fallen human nature inclines us to be self-centered.

The Science of Humility

As with most of the virtues discussed in this book, humility can be considered a state or a trait. State humility occurs in the context of a particular moment and situation, whereas trait humility is a general way of approaching the world. Even a highly narcissistic person may have moments of humility, but most of us strive to move beyond states of humility toward the trait.

One of the most comprehensive understandings of trait humility in the social-science literature comes from psychologist June Tangney, who identified six dimensions of humility:

1. Accurate view of oneself (neither too high nor too low)
2. Ability to acknowledge mistakes and limitations
3. Openness to new ideas
4. Keeping one's accomplishments and abilities in perspective
5. Relatively low self-focus
6. Appreciating diverse perspectives[4]

As more scientific studies on humility began emerging, researchers also started narrowing their definitions even while admiring the more comprehensive view that Tangney offered. Most social scientists today agree on the simpler definition of trait humility that I mentioned in the opening paragraph of this chapter:

1. Views self accurately (neither too high nor too low)
2. Considers the other and not just oneself
3. Is teachable; is open to the possibility of being wrong

These three retain much of Tangney's more comprehensive definition, while having the benefit of parsimony. It is easier to remember a three-pronged definition than a definition with six criteria.

In addition to defining a thing, social scientists have to find ways to measure it. This is no easy task when it comes to trait humility,

---

SIDEBAR 4.1
Intellectual Humility

Researcher Stacey McElroy and her colleagues have developed an Intellectual Humility Scale that involves what is called "informant report." In other words, rather than Person A reporting his or her own humility, Person B is answering questions about Person A's intellectual humility.*

The authors conducted four studies to determine reliability and validity for their scale, and they report hopeful results. The scale includes two subscales—one for intellectual arrogance and one for intellectual openness. Examples of items include the following:

> *Intellectual arrogance*: has to have the last word in an argument; acts like a know-it-all
> *Intellectual openness*: seeks out alternative viewpoints; remains open to competing ideas

Remember that humility is generally considered to involve (1) an accurate view of self, (2) an ability to focus on the other, and (3) teachability. The construct of intellectual humility is primarily related to the third facet of humility.

*Stacey E. McElroy et al., "Intellectual Humility: Scale Development and Theoretical Elaborations in the Context of Religious Leadership," *Journal of Psychology and Theology* 42 (2014): 19–30.

---

both because it is a complex construct that is related to many other virtues and because self-report is inherently problematic when measuring humility. Those who are least humble may perceive and report themselves to be very humble. It is quite a lot easier to measure narcissism than humility,[5] and because narcissism is correlated to all sorts of negative personal and interpersonal qualities, one could presume that humility is related to good outcomes. But as discussed earlier, it is not particularly helpful to define humility based on what it is not. Humility is richer and more nuanced than simply being the opposite of narcissism or pride.

A number of scales have attempted to measure humility. Researchers Don Davis and Joshua Hook recently listed fourteen

SIDEBAR 4.2

Relational Humility

Don Davis and his colleagues developed a way to measure relational humility.* As with the Intellectual Humility Scale (see sidebar 4.1), the Relational Humility Scale uses informant reporting rather than self-report.

The authors report five studies that support their scale, which is composed of three subscales—global humility, superiority, and accurate view of self. Examples of items include the following:

> *Global humility*: He/she is truly a humble person. Even strangers would consider him/her humble.
> *Superiority*: He/she has a big ego; I feel inferior when I am with him/her.
> *Accurate view of self*: He/she knows him-/herself well; he/she is self-aware.

This scale of relational humility assesses the first two components of humility: (1) an accurate view of self and (2) an ability to focus on the other.

*Don E. Davis et al., "Relational Humility: Conceptualizing and Measuring Humility as a Personality Judgment," *Journal of Personality Assessment* 93 (2011): 225–34.

different scales to measure humility, noting that scholars use a variety of approaches.[6] Though the vast majority of scales are self-report, some recent efforts to measure trait humility involve having a knowledgeable informant rate a person's humility (see sidebars 4.1 and 4.2 for examples). Occasionally a study includes both self-report and informant report in assessing humility. Interestingly, correlations between self-reported humility and informant-reported humility are generally quite low, though they are higher when the informant is a romantic partner than when the informant is a coworker, friend, or casual acquaintance.

Because of the measurement challenges, the science of humility lags behind that of some of the other virtues discussed in this book. Still, there is enough evidence to link humility with health

in various ways. Greater humility is associated with greater physical health, greater mental health (self-esteem, gratitude, forgiveness), academic performance, job performance, forgivingness,
generosity, and helpfulness.[7] Humble people experience more
positive romantic relationships than others,[8] form and repair
social bonds more readily than others,[9] are less anxious about
death,[10] are more compassionate,[11] and experience less spiritual
struggle.[12]

It appears that humility is good for us, which will likely make
people interested in becoming more humble, but is this even possible? Can people learn to become more humble, or is it a relatively determined personality trait by the time a person reaches
adulthood? The short answer is, we don't know. Two studies have
been reported, and with mixed results. Caroline Lavelock and her
colleagues tested the effectiveness of a humility workbook with
university students and found modest improvement in humility,
forgivingness, and patience.[13] In contrast, Andrew Cuthbert and
his colleagues found very little effect for a humility intervention
with church leaders.[14] I describe this study in more detail later in
the chapter.

To summarize, humility is conceptualized in three parts: an
accurate view of self, being able to focus on the other, and teachability. The science of humility has been hindered by measurement
challenges, but we can be fairly confident that humility is good for
a person's mental, physical, and relational health. It is less clear
whether people can become more humble with effort.

Moving toward a Christian View of Humility

Christianity has much to offer the serious study of humility. In
his classic book on theological anthropology, Anthony Hoekema
describes how humans are created to be in relationship with God,
others, self, and nature.[15] Each of these reflects a Christian contribution to the understanding of humility.

In Relation to God

A contemporary adage is "There is a God, and it's not me." This is helpful to remember in an age when self-promotion is prominent, and a festering self-loathing sometimes seems to be the only alternative. Neither extreme is humble, and neither allows us to follow the great commandment, to love God with our whole selves.

The virtue of humility reminds us that we are the creatures, deeply loved by our Creator. The word "submission" has fallen out of favor in recent decades, but if we are to fully understand our creaturely relationship to God, we need the concept of submission. These days it is so natural, and some would even say healthy, to shake our fists at God when life goes sideways. There are benefits to this, including the willingness to be brutally honest with God about our disappointments. King David and the other psalmists certainly did their share of lamenting in the Old Testament, but that was always in the context of acknowledging submission to God, even when life felt confusing. Today it seems much lamenting reflects our failure to humble ourselves before God more than a genuine desire to know and be known by God. The Old Testament character Job had more reason to complain to God than most of us, and did so (mostly) in a respectful way. But when he overlooked his creatureliness, God reminded him:

Then the LORD answered Job from the whirlwind:

> "Who is this that questions my wisdom
>   with such ignorant words?
> Brace yourself like a man,
>   because I have some questions for you, and you must
>   answer them.
> Where were you when I laid the foundations of the earth?
>   Tell me, if you know so much.
> Who determined its dimensions
>   and stretched out the surveying line?

> What supports its foundations,
>   and who laid its cornerstone
> as the morning stars sang together
>   and all the angels shouted for joy?" (Job 38:1–7)

We may have given up on the word "submission," largely because it has been so abused to assert dominance by one over the other, but we cannot fully engage in a relationship with our loving, gracious God without reclaiming the submissive nature of humility. Then, as we practice humility toward God, we can begin to understand what it means to "submit to one another out of reverence for Christ" (Eph. 5:21).

Jesus is the center of the Christian faith, the full image of God revealed in human form, and the perfect picture of humility. "He gave up his divine privileges; he took the humble position of a slave and was born as a human being" (Phil. 2:7). It is this image of kenosis, or self-emptying, that the apostle Paul refers to when asking his readers to submit to one another.

The Gospel of John is more a theological look at the life of Jesus than are the other three (synoptic) Gospels. Theologians refer to John as a "view from above" because of its theological nature. The word "humility" doesn't show up, but the idea is painted all through the Gospel account. Reflecting Jesus as portrayed in the Gospel of John, Andrew Murray wrote over a century ago about this stunning portrayal of humility.

> In the Gospel of John we have the inner life of our Lord laid open to us. Jesus speaks frequently of His relation to the Father, of the motives by which He is guided, of His consciousness of the power and spirit in which He acts. Though the word humble does not occur, we shall nowhere in Scripture see so clearly wherein His humility consisted. . . . He took the place of entire subordination, and gave God the honor and the glory which is due to Him.[16]

This is no weak-willed, spineless sort of humility. Jesus taught pointedly, even offensively. All through the Sermon on the Mount

(Matt. 5–7) we see a teacher with confidence and clarity, but we also see teachings that called people to confront their prideful ways and to love God and neighbor.

In Relation to Others

One of the great contributions Christianity offers to the study of humility is the place of community. This can be observed in two dimensions. First, there is the horizontal dimension of community experienced in current relationships. As people care for one another in loving and supportive ways, they are both reflecting God's image and exercising humility. Loving neighbor as self is a hallmark of Christian virtue, part of the second great commandment Jesus taught, and also central to the definitions of humility considered earlier in this chapter.

Church is no perfect place, as we are reminded continually in news reports and cinematic representations, but in those church communities where people are more or less successful in setting aside selfish desires so that they can truly love and learn from one another, the beauty of Christ and the power of humility are evident. My church community recently helped a Muslim refugee family from Syria settle into the United States, providing transportation, friendship, travel reimbursement, and leads for employment. It was a beautiful thing to watch and be part of, and similar stories could be shared about thousands of congregations throughout the world. Telling this kind of good news about the church is as important as holding the church accountable for its mistakes.

Another sort of Christian community happens vertically as a historical community, established through many centuries of Christian thought. Though I do not personally know Augustine or Aquinas or Teresa of Ávila, Martin Luther or Ulrich Zwingli, Jonathan Edwards or Henri Nouwen or Mother Teresa, they have been part of a historical community that shapes the way I think and feel and perceive the world. They, and thousands of others, have shaped the way we Christians understand our faith, and therefore I owe them an incredible debt of gratitude. Christian humility calls us to recognize the wisdom of the pioneers who have gone before us.

A new positive psychology literature is emerging on spiritual humility, which entails holding our certainties loosely and being open to change. On one hand, I am drawn to this literature because indeed our spiritual notions have been used to justify all sorts of hatred and evil over the centuries. We need to hold our ideas somewhat lightly, knowing that we are finite and frail in our ability to discern the truth. On the other hand, I fear that we sometimes portray spiritual humility as requiring an absence of conviction, when Jesus does not. One can become so open, so flexible about matters of faith, that in the process we become quite prideful about ignoring the centuries of intelligent Christian saints who have gone before us and hammered out intricate doctrines to help us understand the nature of God, humanity, and salvation. True spiritual humility must leave room for both openness and deep conviction, for both contemporary and historical community.

In Relation to Nature

Murray begins his classic book on humility by recalling: "When God created the universe, it was with the one object of making the creature partaker of His perfection and blessedness, and so showing forth in it the glory of His love and wisdom and power."[17] And so it is that the universe around us still invites us to experience God's abundant goodness and blessing.

Seeing nature as a servant to be mastered leads us to one set of conclusions about how we fuel our transportation, treat our forests and water, grow our food, and treat the plants and animals around us, and it reflects something that lacks humility. In contrast, seeing nature as reflecting God's perfection and blessedness calls us into a different sort of relationship, more humble and cautious, when considering the world and its resources.

Three times a day (or more) most of us have opportunity to experience God's blessedness through the food we eat—and perhaps to grow in humility as well. Do I eat as if creation is my slave, providing the fuel I need to gulp down whatever I choose to eat in order to feel happy, satiated, and energized for what comes next, or do I see meals as an opportunity to reflect gratefully on God's sustaining presence and goodness in all creation? We may say grace before we eat, but in our food do we see the grace of Christ, the one who "existed before anything else, and . . . holds all creation together" (Col. 1:17)? Norman Wirzba, author of *Food and Faith: A Theology of Eating*, refers to food as God's love made nutritious.[18] This reflects a humble understanding of ourselves in relation to God's creation—and a great way to eat.

Lisa and I run a small farm in the summers, based on a community-supported-agriculture model. We grow about seventy-five fruits and vegetables for about twenty families who come once a week to fill up a crate with sustainable, locally grown food. Whenever I feel humility challenged, I simply reflect on how difficult it is to keep flea beetles from attacking our broccoli leaves, or aphids off the cabbage, or squirrels out of the lettuce. This quickly reminds me that I am not in charge of the universe and can't even master my small slice of farmland very well without resorting to synthetic chemicals that would kill our bees and the microbes the soil desperately needs. So we choose to grow with organic methods, doing whatever we can to keep the so-called pests at bay. But I am telling only half the story when I mention pests, because the other part, and the more glorious one, is observing the beauty and grace of how food grows from the earth. When the sweet corn pops through the soil to reach toward the sun, or when I pass by a mature tomato plant and breathe in the amazing aroma of fresh tomatoes, or when I see the verdant green of June lettuce, then I also feel humble as I realize how grand this rhythm of life is and how much grander its Creator. Each ear of corn, every tomato and head of lettuce, is God's love made nutritious. Lisa's book

SIDEBAR 4.3

Facing Life's Struggles

During a season fraught with particularly difficult life circumstances, Celeste Jones, a colleague of mine, wrote an essay (unpublished) about the process of self-confrontation and humility, and she gave me permission to include it here.

> There are so many hard things that happen in life. One day your life is going along predictably, and the next day your sense of security is washed away without warning, leaving you scrambling for footing. And when you're scrambling for footing, it's hard to see your surroundings very clearly, let alone anything in the distance. And usually, scrambling means you're about ready for a painful crash. The good life feels very far away and your chances at it seem lost, and even if you are able to locate the good life, you don't know how to get there. You don't know how to even "be" anymore. And you worry and groan and ache and cry and angst and you do all those things over and over and over until the night comes. On good nights, you are able to get yourself to sleep.
>
> But regardless of whether you sleep or stay up angst-ing all night, the morning always comes. The sun comes up every day, like an open invitation to come to life again. A new chance, every single day. The morning asks you to put your clothes on, snuggle your children, feed them breakfast, walk the dog, and get going on the duties of the day. Some days you carry out all your duties while your head is still spinning with angst. Some days,

To the Table explores this in far more detail than I am able to go into here.[19]

One doesn't need to be a farmer to foster this sort of humility in relation to creation. Go to the ocean, climb part or all of a mountain, hike through an old-growth forest, sit at the base of a waterfall, look at the stars. Whenever I do these things, it helps put me back where I belong—not at the center of it all, but as a creature of a lavish God who delights in showing us beauty and love.

In Relation to Self

Finally, Hoekema suggests that a right relationship with God, others, and nature presumes a right relationship with self. At the while you are on your walk, you notice a beautiful meadow of tall grass and make a hideout with your children, catching ladybugs and playing hide and seek. Moments of the good life unfold unexpectedly. But when the evening slows down and the children are put in bed and the house is all tidied, the relentless angst finds you again, at least for the night.

How does one survive these seasons? What if these seasons stretch into years? People who figure these things out are my heroes. I know these people when I meet them, those who have been humbled by great suffering. They have a focus and centeredness that can only be forged through the burning fires of anguish. Not everyone makes it. Many times, we refuse to put ourselves in situations to be burned. We avoid hard things or deny their existence. Other times, we find ways to protect ourselves from the fire, we gird ourselves with fireproof gear so that the fire can't touch us. And all that gear can get heavy. Still other times, we point our effort toward putting out the fire, solving small problems that feel like the causes. But there are some people who are strong enough (or crazy enough?) to let themselves be burned, to lean into their pain and let it do its work, even if the work takes a while. And when we're able to allow ourselves to burn, to look into the face of our pain, we become something much stronger, healthier, more resilient, more honest, and more humble than when we began. We become people who can sit with other people in their own pain and suffering and not try to fix it for them or figure it out for them or make them feel better. We become people who can just be. And maybe that's the good life.

heart of a Christian anthropology is the paradox that we are of immense value—created in the image of God, and loved so deeply that God refuses to leave us alone in our struggles—and simultaneously broken, twisted, distorted by the brokenness of all creation. Like all creation, we groan in our brokenness (Rom. 8:23), both for our personal shortcomings and for the general suffering that afflicts every cranny in the world around us.

The depth of God's grace can be grasped only when we understand this paradox of how much God loves us, how much we struggle, and how we are lovingly called to a more abundant way of living. We can pound our chest in pride if we choose, as champion athletes sometimes do, or we can settle into a long awareness of this paradoxical life where we are beautifully made, deeply flawed, loved beyond measure, and called to grow.

Brooks captures this well in his book about humility, suggesting that truly humble people use a particular metaphor of the internal life:

> This is the metaphor of self-confrontation. They are more likely to assume that we are all deeply divided selves, both splendidly endowed and deeply flawed—that we each have certain talents but also certain weaknesses. And if we habitually fall for those temptations and do not struggle against the weaknesses in ourselves, then we will gradually spoil some core piece of ourselves. We will not be as good, internally, as we want to be. We will fail in some profound way. For people of this sort, the external drama up the ladder of success is important, but the inner struggle against one's own weaknesses is the central drama of life. . . . Truly humble people are engaged in a great effort to magnify what is best in themselves and defeat what is worst, to become strong in the weak places.[20]

From a Christian vantage point, I would add that this is not just a white-knuckled effort at self-improvement, but a firm belief that God is present through our struggles. We can spend our lives denying our divided selves if we choose, but to do so is to engage in decades of avoidance and self-deception. Another alternative is to lean into our struggles and weaknesses, to affirm that God is working to help us become strong in those weak places, and that humility is found amidst the honesty of the internal struggle.

Humility's Telos

All through this book on virtue I have mused on the great commandments offered by Jesus in Matthew 22. To consider the fully functioning person in relation to humility, I return again to this passage.

Who asked Jesus the question, "Teacher, which is the most important commandment in the law of Moses?" (v. 36)? It was a chest-thumping linebacker, a narcissistic politician, a self-absorbed religious personality. All of these embody a me-centered approach to the world, where I am simply the best and you are not. The person asking Jesus the question was a religious expert who set out to trap Jesus, probably threatened by the crowds following Jesus.

Confronted with the smallness of petty human jealousy, Jesus answered by offering the telos of humility—a picture of what a whole, fully functioning, flourishing human being might look like. It's the one who loves God with his or her whole being and loves neighbor as self.

This is the essence of humility. It doesn't require self-deprecation or self-loathing, but it does call us to get ourselves out of the line of vision. We live in a time when mirrors line walls of health clubs and advertisers tell us every day what we deserve, and Jesus simply tells us to stand aside, to become self-forgetful enough that we can focus our attention on God and neighbor. And when that happens, as it sometimes does in the context of Christian community, we catch a glimpse of humility's telos.

Some friends of ours face a decades-long heartbreak with a child addicted to drugs. They have helped in every way imaginable, but the power of addiction persists, and they struggle every day to know how best to help this child they love so deeply. A few weeks ago we ran into our friends at a local restaurant, talked a few moments, and then went on with our meals. Lisa turned to me later and said, "I want to put together a crate of food for them." And so she did. She drove by their house the following day with a crate of organic produce, eggs from our hens, some freshly baked cookies, and a card expressing our support. In one regard it was such a small thing—no one gave up a kidney to save a life or stepped in front of a speeding car or took a bullet or even spent much money. It was just a box of food gathered from our gardens, the hen house, and in the kitchen. Lisa probably didn't even think of it as humility, but that's what it was: stepping aside from self-interest, noticing the other, and offering food as God's love made nutritious. Our friends were deeply touched and blessed, and in the process we all saw a small glimpse of how humility calls us together.

Scientific and Christian Humility, Side by Side

Thus far the science of humility has focused mostly on how to define and measure it, which is a prerequisite for the serious scientific study that is yet to come. As described earlier, we know that humility is good for us in various ways, but we don't know enough yet to understand the nuanced relationships between health and humility. A common understanding in the scientific community is that humble people see themselves relatively accurately, attend well to others, and are teachable.

Christianity has been considering humility much longer than social scientists, so it's not surprising that the Christian tradition has much to offer to those interested in the topic. Consistent with a scientific definition, Jesus—the exemplar of self-emptying—both demonstrates and teaches humility in the command to love neighbor as self.

The John Templeton Foundation grant that I have referred to in several chapters of this book funded a dissertation by Andrew Cuthbert, a doctoral student at Wheaton College, to look at humility in the context of a church community.[21] Specifically, Andrew and his supervisor, Ward Davis, attempted to increase humility in a group of leaders that were part of a large Christian congregation. The leaders went through a four-week workbook that involved sixteen daily exercises to promote humility. Andrew and the team of scholars he worked with administered a number of scales both before and after the humility intervention and administered a similar set of measures to a comparison group. He measured humility both by self-report and by having an informant report on the humility of his participants.

Before describing Andrew's results, I should mention what one expert reviewer of his project wrote prior to the study. This reviewer has been highly involved in humility research, especially related to the measurement of humility. He expressed doubts as to whether humility can or should be taught through a short-term explicit intervention. Do we become humble by doing humility workbooks and homework, or is it more the result of living a good-hearted and godly life over many years? He predicted that Andrew wouldn't find much in his four-week intervention study, despite the findings reported by Lavelock and her colleagues, described earlier.[22]

It turned out the expert reviewer was right. Almost no changes were evident as a result of the four-week humility intervention, though a couple findings were intriguing. One is that the Global Humility Subscale of the Relational Humility Scale (see sidebar 4.2) was higher after the intervention than before for those in the intervention group, but not for those in the comparison group. This was the change that Andrew was expecting, but it showed up on only one subscale of his various humility scales. The other intriguing finding is that self-report and informant-report were more consistent for his intervention group at the end of the study than they were for the comparison group. This raises the possibility that the humility training helped participants to see themselves more like others see them.

The science of humility is in its infancy, while humility has been a topic considered in Christianity for many centuries. Science and faith may not be equal talking partners on this topic, but both have contributions to offer to the conversation.

Redeeming Humility

Both as a way to summarize this chapter and to press forward with what possibilities lie ahead, let's consider how we might redeem the construct of humility in our conversing, teaching, counseling, and living.

Learning from Positive Psychology

One of the most important contributions of positive psychology is defining humility apart from what it is not. Though it is clear that humility contrasts with pride and narcissism, most of the scientific work has looked at humility directly, for its merits as a virtue. We have some initial measurement tools, involving both self-report and report from a knowledgeable informant. It also seems clear from various studies that humility enhances relational and personal health.

We don't yet know whether humility can be taught in short-term interventions. Two studies have been reported where participants work through a humility workbook. In one study people appeared to become more humble, and in the other very few differences were noted between the humility group and the comparison group. This will be an important frontier for continued conversation and re-search. It seems possible that trait humility is "caught" more than "taught," learned over a lifetime by observing family members, friends, and people in communities of faith. If so, then science is a difficult way to learn about the acquisition of humility because our studies rarely extend over a lifetime of learning.

What Can Christian Thought Offer to Humility?

The Christian contributions to topics of pride and humility are enormous. I have only scratched the surface in this brief chapter. David Brooks, though not writing from an explicitly Christian perspective, seems to understand the issues at stake very well, and so I have quoted him frequently. A Christian worldview calls us to a continual place of self-appraisal and self-confrontation. The self I am is not the fully functioning self that I strive to become. This is quite a countercultural notion in an age when self-promotion is the norm and is often even seen as healthy. Sometimes it seems we even consider it virtuous. In contrast, a Christian worldview suggests that the self is not to be trusted very much because it is tainted and twisted with selfish desire and ambition. Instead of trusting the self, we learn to confront the self and to find our greatest source of hope and meaning not so much in the self but in the love of God and neighbor. The great ground of hope from a Christian worldview is not that we are special or wonderful or even above average, but that we are deeply loved by a gracious God who works relentlessly to draw us into an abiding relationship. In the context of that secure, safe relationship with God we are invited to similar relationships with one another. And here, nestled in a web of meaningful relationships that reflect God's grace and the humility of Jesus, we find healing, hope, and all sorts of human flourishing.

The Church Can Benefit from the Science of Humility

Throughout the book I have argued that the church needs positive psychology in order to foster a meaningful and peacemaking dialogue between faith and science, and to remain relevant in a society that increasingly looks to science for truth. In addition, the church can take particular findings from science to help contextualize and respond to challenges of twenty-first-century Western culture. One example of this is found in the area of divine struggle, where we as humans experience frustration, disappointment, and anger toward God because of the bad things that happen to and around us.

Divine struggle has always been an issue in the church, described with various names (e.g., theodicy, the problem of pain, lament). Godly biblical writers, including King David, the man "after [God's] own heart" (1 Sam. 13:14), experienced and expressed divine struggle. The biblical writers asked hard questions of God and lamented their struggles, but in the context of a secure relationship with the divine. Today, divine struggle seems to be a major reason people are leaving a relationship with God—or at least with the church.

Hidden in the emerging humility literature is a little-known study that seems to have great importance in this regard. Researchers Joshua Grubbs and Julie Exline identified two forms of divine struggle: anger at God and religious fear/guilt.[23] They found humility to be robustly and negatively related to anger at God even when controlling for other personality traits. There is also a negative relationship between humility and religious fear/guilt, though not as strong as the relationship with anger at God. The more humble we are, the less we experience divine struggle.

This has huge implications for how we conduct ourselves in the twenty-first-century church. So often when a person (often a young person) has doubts about God, we pair that person with a natural apologist (typically an older person). The apologist offers cognitive arguments for why God is still good despite life's suffering. The young person listens politely and then typically leaves the church anyway. But given what we know about humility, perhaps it would be much better to pair the questioning pilgrim with the most naturally humble person we can find. The humble person may have less certainty to offer the quester, but the humility will likely rub off in some winsome sorts of ways, and with humility the divine struggle may subside.

Another way we churchgoers can learn from the science of humility relates to the construct of cultural humility. Some of the same researchers who have studied relational humility and intellectual humility have extended the ideas to consider how we interact with those who are culturally different from us.[24] Many of the leading positive psychology researchers studying cultural humility are committed Christians who long to see the church be a place where we embody humility in relation to human diversity. Most congregations continue to be quite culturally segregated, which means our efforts to become more welcoming and diverse are critically important. Humility, with its focus on the other and on being open and teachable, is a great way to start the process of becoming more culturally welcoming in our faith communities.

Humility in Christian Counseling

Finally, humility research has implications for pastoral and Christian counselors. I began this chapter by mentioning the historic antithetical relationship between pride (as vice) and humility (as virtue). There is much to affirm about this pairing, but it can be deceptive in the counseling office for at least two reasons.

First, counselors are familiar with prideful clients. We call them narcissists and are often overwhelmed by how self-absorbed and superficial they can be. The natural assumption is that we need to teach them greater humility, but then we feel frustrated because all our efforts to do so seem to fail. Experienced counselors know that narcissism is not only a function of pride but is also armor resulting from early wounds. Rather than teaching humility to the narcissistic client, it seems much better to model it by leaning into their stories, pushing ourselves toward exceptional empathy even as our natural tendencies might be to push the arrogant person away because of how distasteful he or she can be. We counselors are called to model humility, even if we sit with people who are struggling to be humble. With exceptional empathy, and over what is sometimes a long period of time, we begin to see a fragile, vulnerable child who was once so deeply wounded that thick armor seemed the only reasonable solution. The armor of pride now pushes people away, but at least it protects the wearer from the vulnerability of being close to another human being.

Second, we sometimes think of self-deprecation as the opposite of pride and thus associate it with humility. The narcissist is proud, and the depressed patient is humble. This dichotomy is quite false and can be a destructive assumption in counseling. Both the narcissist and the depressed patient are caught in a cycle of self-absorption. Humility is not thinking poorly of ourselves, but thinking accurately. We naturally lean to self-esteem-boosting strategies with depressed clients, assuming they just need to think more highly of themselves, but I'm skeptical of how much this helps. It seems more reasonable to help them learn how to stand aside and spend less time thinking about how wounded and sad they may feel. Instead, the sad and depressed person can learn to accept that these feelings will come from time to time, but the feelings do not need to define him or her. Many people, including those who face depression periodically throughout life, are able to define their values and live congruent and productive lives that contribute to the welfare of society. For more on this approach to counseling, see Joshua Knabb's fine book on Acceptance and Commitment Therapy with Christian clients.[25]

Humility is a great conversation topic for science and the church. At this point, the church has the most to offer to the conversation because of centuries of reflection and thought that have gone into the topic. The science is nascent, but important to consider, especially with regard to implications for those who are struggling with God and those in our counseling offices.

5

∎∎∎∎∎∎∎∎

Hope

I could subtitle this chapter "Three and a Half Stars for Positive Psychology." The study of hope in recent decades, as with so many topics covered in this book, has helped social scientists consider what goes right with people. This is a welcome relief after psychologists have spent so many decades studying what goes wrong. We have operational definitions for hope now, and hundreds of studies showing its benefits. Hip, hip, and almost hurray.

Why the muted enthusiasm? When I read the science of hope, I have that nagging sense that some essential part of virtue has been left behind. So yes, let's study hope and celebrate it, and live longer because we do, but let's also work to redeem a Christian understanding of hope at the same time.

Scientists have different definitions of hope, but many of them go back to the seminal work of C. R. Snyder and his colleagues in the 1980s. This understanding of hope involves (1) feeling optimistic that my future can be better than the present, (2) identifying pathways to help me move from where I am now to where I want to be, and (3) having a sense of motivation to make it so. Put another way, hopeful people have a vision for what is possible, a way to change, and a will to change. Mostly I like this definition. When I think of a twenty-year-old high school dropout from a disadvantaged school who decides to get a GED, enroll in community college, and make something better of her life, or his, then I love the definition. When I imagine the sedentary adolescent who decides to get active and start eating healthier foods, it's a great definition. Or when a newly divorced person decides it's time to move past the stifling bitterness and depression of intense loss and build a better future, then this is an excellent way to understand hope.

But sometimes this definition wears thin. Palm Sunday seems hopeful enough, but a Christian understanding of hope takes us beyond palm branches and hosannas, deep into the valley of despair.

If hope is merely being optimistic that the future will be better than the present, and that we can do something to make it that way, I wonder what I should say to the friends in my adult Sunday school class who are suffering in various ways. One person just lost his wife to leukemia. Several are fighting cancer for the first or second time. Others have had strokes or are caring for spouses who have suffered one. Another almost lost his life with a bout of bacterial meningitis and subsequent sepsis and is having to relearn the basic motor skills of life, such as how to walk. One couple just lost a grandchild in a terrible accident. I think any definition of hope that overlooks the role of suffering would seem pallid and trite to these friends. Still, I see joy in their eyes and witness the compassion they have for one another. I think they have each experienced some bigger version of hope than what we are studying in positive psychology laboratories. All this suffering—and more—has affected a class of about forty people who meet together week after week. When we meet, broken and aging as we are, the room is filled with laughter and love and hope that could never be measured on a social science rating scale.

Yes, there may well be a bright future, but this is no straight-upward trajectory where every day is slightly better than the day before. Resurrection requires death. For hope to work in the real world, it will need to help us find meaning amidst great suffering.

In David Brooks's fine book about humility, mentioned frequently in chapter 4, he notes:

> The people in this book led diverse lives. Each one of them exemplifies one of the activities that lead to character. But there is one pattern that recurs: They had to go down to go up. They had to descend into the valley of humility to climb to the heights of character. . . . The everyday self-deceptions and illusions of self-mastery were shattered. . . . But then the beauty began. In the valley of humility they learned to quiet the self. Only by quieting the self could they see the world clearly. Only by quieting the self could they understand other people and accept what they are offering. When they had quieted themselves, they had opened up space for grace to flood in.[1]

Though the word "hope" doesn't appear in Brooks's index, I think it's a book closely related to hope. By entering the valley of humility and only then discovering the grace that others offer, we experience a deep sort of hope that "lives well" amidst the complexities and turbulence of life.

A Christian view of hope traverses through Holy Week and somehow finds hope in it all. Yes, the hope is about Easter, but it shows up before Easter morning. As theologian Simon Kwan writes, "Real hope can only be adequately understood against an eschatological horizon."[2] Eschatology is sometimes reduced to the expectation of heaven—the happily-ever-after life—but as wonderful as the hope of heaven is, theologian Jürgen Moltmann reminds us that "from first to last, and not merely in the epilogue, Christianity is eschatology, is hope, forward looking and forward moving, and therefore also revolutionizing and transforming the present."[3]

Some have distinguished between what has been called particularized hope (focused on a specific goal or outcome) and generalized hope (a more general sense that all is well, even when particular circumstances or outcomes seem to argue otherwise).

To the Christian, an eschatological horizon creates a generalized positive expectancy for the nature and character of God, in this life and beyond. It is not tightly bound to particular outcomes, but to God. Somewhere on the eschatological horizon—viewed through our finite awareness of God's unfathomable grace—faith, hope, and love abound.

We scientists tend to think of hope as a construct, some definable alloy of cognition and goal-oriented behavior that can be measured with self-report scales, but what if hope isn't so much a construct as it is a relationship? And here is where you're expecting me to say that hope is found in relationship with Jesus. Well, yes, I'll say it—Jesus is the essence of hope for Christians, the image of God made fully known—but hope ripples out of that center into millions of persons scattered throughout history and around the world. When I see hope in the eyes of the suffering Sunday school friends I just described, I am seeing Jesus but I am also seeing my friends—virtuous people who have been transformed by decades of their own faithful Christian living in communities of hope-inspiring people and in the abiding presence of generations who have gone before them. They understand the valley of humility, so they can understand grace. And in grace they find hope. It's not so much a particular hope; each of the cancer patients I worship with week after week would say his or her future is uncertain, and one has recently called in hospice to help her negotiate her final days. Rather, it is a generalized hope, affirming the loving and gracious character of the people they know and have known in the past, and of God, from whom all blessings and all virtues flow.

The Science of Hope

Lest it sound like I'm opposed to the scientific study of hope, that is not at all the case. I'm grateful for science and for the science of hope. Sometimes the definitions and findings seem a bit anemic to me, especially when I'm considering the larger ecclesial context of

Christian hope through the centuries, but still, I'm an enthusiastic social scientist. Science is the language of the day, and if we in the church want to remain relevant, we need to keep up with the dialect, even if it deserves only three and a half stars. So here's a brief and incomplete summary of what we know about hope.

Hope involves a vision for how to move forward (pathway) and the motivation to get there (agency). Not surprisingly, this is related to many positive health outcomes.[4] People with relatively high levels of hope tend to exercise more than others as well as engage in other disease-prevention activities. They participate in fewer high-risk sexual activities than others and are less prone to self-injury and suicidal ideation. Hopeful individuals also eat more fruit and vegetables than others, and they cope better when they get sick, whether from a burn injury, spinal cord injury, fibromyalgia, arthritis, or blindness. They adhere better to treatment and cope better with pain than low-hope individuals do, which necessitates a brief story from Shane Lopez, a leading expert on hope.

In his book *Making Hope Happen*, Lopez tells the story of his colleague and mentor, C. R. Snyder, who once appeared on *Good Morning America* to discuss hope.[5] Snyder invited three of the show's personalities—Charlie Gibson, Tim Johnson, and Tony Perkins—to put their right fists into a tank of ice water for as long as they could stand it. This, by the way, is a common test used by social scientists to assess pain tolerance. Interestingly, the order in which they gave up holding their hand in the cold water was precisely the order that Snyder predicted, based on a hope scale he had given each of them prior to the show. In case you're interested, Charlie Gibson was the most hopeful—and the most pain tolerant—of the three.

I recall a similar experiment with my family when my three children were young. As a family, we headed to the park on a Sunday afternoon and ended up having a silly leg-lifting contest. The rules of the contest, which I established with a clear eye toward winning, were that we all lie on the grass and hold our heels six inches above the ground, with legs straight, and that we hold this posture as long as physically possible. The last to give up would be the winner. Most of my family members were sensible enough to let their feet drop to the ground before the pain became unmanageable. Soon it was just me and my youngest daughter, Megan Anna. She moaned out in pain, but kept her feet raised above the ground until I finally gave up. That gave me an idea—maybe we could try the best two out of three, rather than declaring a winner right away. Again, the same thing happened. Megan Anna persisted through great moaning and won the contest. I remember asking her how she did it and being quite stunned at her seven-year-old reply: "Once I figured out it was okay to hurt, then it was easy." Megan Anna and Charlie Gibson would likely both score high on a hope scale, at least with regard to the agency dimension. And she will need it as she is embarking on a rigorous doctoral program while she and Luke (her husband) continue to provide loving care for their two children.

Life—and hope—is more complicated than how long one can keep a hand in ice water or hold up one's legs in the park, so it's important to remember that hope also involves a vision for the future. As a hopeless person has a vision fade, the hopeful person finds a way to hold on. This is reminiscent of Viktor Frankl, the author of *Man's Search for Meaning*, who survived Auschwitz and other concentration camps and was fond of quoting Friedrich Nietzsche: "He who has a why to live can bear almost any how." Though I'm not inclined to quote Nietzsche much myself, I deeply admire Frankl and his amazing capacity to maintain hope amidst the most horrendous conditions one might imagine.

To whatever extent hope promotes a sense of purpose for life, we can expect even more health benefits. In a recent review and meta-analysis, Randy Cohen and his colleagues reported robust evidence that having a high sense of life purpose reduces risk for various sorts of life-threatening illnesses and cardiovascular events.[6] Various mental health benefits have also been associated with hope. Hopeful people experience more positive emotions and fewer negative emotions than others. Hopeful college students report being more energized, inspired, and confident than their lower-hope peers, and are less likely to be depressed. Similarly, among older adults hope is associated with life satisfaction and well-being. And those who are hopeful have closer relationships with others; they report giving and receiving more social support than those who have less hope.[7]

In addition to health outcomes, individuals with high levels of hope perform better on the job than others. Rebecca Reichard and her colleagues published an extensive meta-analysis of hope at work and reported substantial work-outcome-related benefits for hopeful employees.[8] Similarly, hopeful students attend class more often and achieve better academically than less-hopeful students, even after controlling for differences in intelligence.[9]

Are you convinced? Even if we may want to quibble some with the definition of hope used in these studies, the science of hope is compelling and consistent. Hope is associated with all sorts of good things.

Though most research linking hope and health is related to the cognitive model developed by Snyder and his colleagues, others have studied hope from a more comprehensive perspective. For example, Anthony Scioli and Henry Biller perceive hope to come from a network of subsystems involving four channels: mastery, attachment, survival, and spirituality.[10] Drawing from various disciplines (e.g., psychology, philosophy, theology, and nursing), Scioli and colleagues view hope as a "future-directed, four-channel emotion network, constructed from biological, psychological, and social resources."[11] This more complex theory of hope fits well with the complex conversations that show up in the counseling office and presumably in everyday language.[12]

Moving toward a Christian View of Hope

In *The Road to Character*, Brooks observes that we now live in a culture he calls "The Big Me." Self-interest has become the ubiquitous

SIDEBAR 5.1
The Big Me

In a 2015 National Public Radio interview, *New York Times* columnist David Brooks had this to say about "The Big Me."

> My favorite statistic about this is that in 1950 the Gallup organization asked high school seniors: Are you a very important person? And in 1950, 12 percent said yes. They asked again in 2005 and it was 80 percent who said they were a very important person. So we live in a culture that encourages us to be big about ourselves, and I think the starting point of trying to build inner goodness is to be a little bit smaller about yourself.

Just in case a picture really is worth a thousand words, here's what Brooks reported in graphical display:

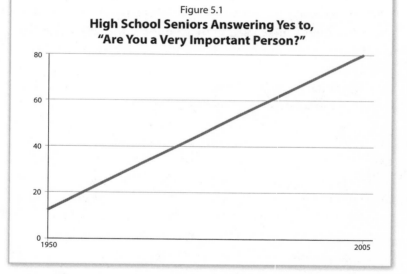

Figure 5.1
**High School Seniors Answering Yes to,
"Are You a Very Important Person?"**

filter through which the ideas and events of life are understood. It's so normal now that most often we don't even feel apologetic or embarrassed about being so self-focused. This cultural assumption seems quite evident when it comes to the science of hope.

Consider two dimensions of The Big Me in the positive psychology of hope. First, as is true of the science of virtue in general, most research about hope focuses on how it can help the individual who hopes. If I read the science and am persuaded by it, I may come to hope because it is good for me, just as I forgive and experience gratitude for similar reasons. Second, the very definition of hope—at least as studied by social scientists—is founded on something I muster for myself. If you're in a tough situation, and you're a hopeful person, then you have the vision and tenacity to move forward and make your life better. I have no question that this sort of hope is a good quality in humans, but it falls short when it comes to a comprehensive view of virtue.

In their classic handbook introducing the scientific study of virtue, Christopher Peterson and Martin E. P. Seligman borrowed heavily from religious traditions in identifying virtues, but then tended to remove most religious language when describing the virtues. Removing religion makes some sense from a scientific vantage point, but it calls into question how the virtues may look different than they did in their original faith-based context. Here is, more or less, Peterson and Seligman's entire treatment of the religious basis of hope:

> The term *hope* has a long history, figuring prominently in Judeo-Christian discourse and naming one of the chief theological virtues (along with faith and charity). Throughout the history of hope, it has referred to positive expectations about matters that have a reasonable likelihood of coming to pass. In principle, there is a darker side of hope, to be sure, but it usually is a qualified version (blind hope, false hope, foolish hope, and so on). Whether this darker side of hope actually exists is debatable.[13]

Notice the not-so-subtle implication that religion may have brought us some good ideas but that we need to be careful not to be blinded by faith. While it is true that religion can be used to mask reality, it is also true that viewing any virtue outside its faith-based context can lead to a different sort of blindness. The Big Me doesn't see very well.

The Big Me centers hope in myself—my vision, my motivation, my tenacity, my goals—whereas a Christian understanding of hope is centered in Jesus. As most of us clamor to figure out how special or worthy we are, or how fairly we are being treated, or perhaps how long we can hold our hand in a bucket of ice water, Jesus climbs the hill with a cross on his back, suffers the death of a criminal, slowly suffocating to demonstrate the fullness of divine, self-offering love. There is only one human being who ever had the right to claim superiority over others, and what does he do? He dies an innocent man, forgives us our enduring pride, and calls us to walk alongside as his friend. Hope, to the Christian, is centered here, in relationship with one who is filled with self-offering love and who calls us into similar relationships with one another.

While at Wheaton College, I had the distinct privilege of team teaching with Walter Elwell, a world-renowned New Testament scholar. Walter used to say to our students, all of whom were studying to become psychologists, "As Christians we never have the option of giving up hope." Every time I heard Walter say this, it carried a sense of profound significance. Here were women and men who would be sitting in prisons evaluating and treating those facing life sentences for horrendous crimes, working with families whose children have been removed, talking with adolescents and adults who have faced unspeakable trauma and evil. Into this reality, Walter spoke these words about the permanence of hope. If hope is about me and my ability to overcome whatever circumstances life brings my way, then I question the veracity of what Walter had to say, but if hope is centered in Christ, and therefore in the relentless and lavish love of God, then Walter's words settle deep into my soul and cause me an inexplicable sense of peace and, well, hope.

Lest I be too harsh on the science of hope, I should affirm the place of motivation and tenacity that is so central to cognitive views of hope. Similarly, a Christian view of hope emphasizes perseverance and steadfastness in the midst of difficult times. Moltmann writes that hope may "yet still remain a piece of sterile theologizing if we fail to attain to the new thought and action that are consequently necessary in our dealings with the things and conditions of this world. As long as hope does not embrace and transform the thought and action of men, it remains topsy-turvy and ineffective."[14] Hope sustains, purifies, inspires, and comforts us even as it protects us from despair and cynicism. As Elwell insisted with our students, Christians hold on to hope even in the most difficult times. To the Christian, for whom the center of hope is outside the self and outside all the possessions a self can acquire, this means that hope can transcend personal loss, tragedy, and even death.

Hope's Telos

Sleep deprivation is tough on me, as it is for many. If I sleep too little one night, I generally function fairly well the next day, but if the same happens the following night, I start to get grumpy on the third day. By the fourth day the world looks gloomy and bleak, and I tend to forget how much I want to be a person of hope. Sometimes my sleep deprivation extends several more days, both because I'm not a great sleeper and because I tend to take on too much and end up working crazy hours to get things finished. (As discussed in the chapter on humility, though we tend to elevate busyness in our society, I do not consider it a virtue. It is a weakness of mine, and I am actively looking for ways to fight against it.)

Here are two ways I have learned to regain hope amidst the hopelessness that settles in with days of sleep deprivation. One way is fortitude. If I stick with whatever project is overwhelming me, just do it, I eventually complete it, feel enormous relief, and get a good night's sleep. Sometimes I'll settle into a pattern of many nights with good sleep. Life seems bright and promising again, and I am able to get there by casting a vision and disciplining myself to get the task done that was keeping me awake. This is the pathways/agency form of hope studied in positive psychology.

A second way to find hope in spite of sleep deprivation is to take a walk with Lisa. We have a number of walking routes around our house, including a two-mile jaunt that takes us uphill and back, passing by sheep and llama, horses and cows, and lots of beautiful fields and plants. If we catch it just right, between Oregon rain clouds, we can enjoy a view of Mount Hood on the way down the hill. We share good conversation, reflecting on the contours of life together. And somehow in this process I recover hope. This, I think, is more like a Christian view of hope—deeply relational and connected with the world around us. To picture this fully, imagine that God often invites us on a walk, just to stroll with us and enjoy the beauty around, to catch up in good conversation and remind us that life is bigger than the things we busy ourselves with. To paraphrase and take some liberties with the powerful words of Israel's King David in Psalm 23, we see that God guides us along right paths and beside peaceful streams, renews us, and even if our walk takes us through the darkest valley, God remains beside us, leading us toward a feast on the holy mountain. And here, walking with Lisa and walking with God, is where I am most likely to experience the fullness of being human. A relational view of hope brings me closer to my telos than a fortitude view of hope, though I believe both are important.

Walking with God is no easy thing, in part because we have become so unfamiliar with God's character. All around I hear people questioning whether God can be good when so many terrible things happen. I grieve this because I believe God wants to be known and has gone to great lengths to make it so. I wonder how God experiences this great unknowing where we attribute the tragic things of this world to God being capricious or unconcerned about the events of our daily lives.

There is a way out of this quagmire, at least to some extent, but it is not a popular way. A great source of hope to the Christian ought to be the doctrine of sin, properly understood. Historically, Christians have believed the cosmos is composed of more than random obstacles calling us to self-motivation and

courage for purposes of self-improvement and living as many
days with as much success as possible. In this Christian view,
the cosmos reflects the struggle between good and evil, and all
of us live under the weight of a broken reality.[15] Even as we long
for something better, we believe that the Christ event (i.e., the
incarnation, life, death, and resurrection of Jesus) assures us
that good will ultimately overcome evil and is in the process of
overcoming evil even now.

> Yet what we suffer now is nothing compared to the glory he will
> reveal to us later. For all creation is waiting eagerly for that future
> day when God will reveal who his children really are. Against its
> will, all creation was subjected to God's curse. But with eager hope,
> the creation looks forward to the day when it will join God's chil-
> dren in glorious freedom from death and decay. For we know that
> all creation has been groaning as in the pains of childbirth right
> up to the present time. And we believers also groan, even though
> we have the Holy Spirit within us as a foretaste of future glory,
> for we long for our bodies to be released from sin and suffering.
> We, too, wait with eager hope for the day when God will give us
> our full rights as his adopted children, including the new bodies
> he has promised us. We were given this hope when we were saved.
> (If we already have something, we don't need to hope for it. But
> if we look forward to something we don't yet have, we must wait
> patiently and confidently.) (Rom. 8:18–25)

I see in my students' generation a loss of this language of sin.
This likely came to be because my generation, and perhaps my
parents' generation also, emphasized the personal nature of sin in
a way that felt more hopeless than hopeful. But careful theological
study has always emphasized that sin is both act and state—the
state meaning that all the world is oppressed and warped by the
weight of a broken creation. And if we lose this understanding of
sin as state, we also lose all explanatory power over human tragedy and suffering. Everywhere we look it seems there is pain and
loss and struggle. The only possibility in a theology without sin

is that God is capricious or powerless or the source of both good and evil. It's difficult to find hope in relationship with such a God.

In *Speaking of Sin*, Barbara Brown Taylor refers to sin as "our only hope," and though Taylor herself may have shifted some in her understanding of theology in recent decades, I find her connection between sin and hope compelling for at least two reasons.[16] First, if we believe in sin, then we can better understand suffering. No, I don't mean there is some simple one-to-one correspondence between a person's sinful behavior and the suffering that person experiences. Since the time of Augustine, and probably before, Christians have understood that terrible things will happen in a world that groans under the weight of sinfulness. No simple formulas can explain how and why people suffer or why some people are asked to endure more suffering than others, but clearly suffering will persist and will visit every human soul in various ways. We can look to Adam and Eve, as Augustine did, however we may understand the historicity of the first humans, but we can also look to ourselves to see that we still eat the forbidden fruit and hide in shame, and every time we do we contribute to the weight of this world's brokenness. We may not have the same moral capacity that the first humans did, because the weight of sin weakens us, but still we are complicit in the human selfishness that ends up hurting every part of our world.

Second, if we exist amidst a great cosmic struggle of good versus evil, and if the same struggle exists inside every human soul, then we can begin to understand the loving, self-offering character of God. Rather than being the source of human suffering, God is a patient, wooing, loving being who will stop at nothing to bring hope to us despite our struggle. Even as the battle rages, and with the promise that good will ultimately triumph over evil, Jesus comes to be with us in our squalor, sweats and bleeds and cries in our midst, shows us the power of virtuous living and dying, and then ultimately demonstrates the resurrection power that is changing the world and that will ultimately defeat the power of all sin.

Just this morning I learned of a woman who kissed her husband good-bye yesterday as he headed to work and who today is a widow because he suffered a sudden aortic rupture. She sat in the hospital during his fourteen-hour surgery saying how much she loves her husband, how desperate she will be without him, and yet how much she trusts God regardless of what happens. Her words may make no sense to most people who hear them, but I think she understands that Christ is suffering alongside her today, as her friends and family are, groaning with her as the weight of this fallen world rests on her shoulders. I'm sure she holds a hope for a future day when she will see her husband again, but even more I think she finds hope in the sustaining presence of the one who understands suffering best of all. She's walking with God and with others who share her understanding of God, through the valley of the shadow of death, and I can't think of better companions in a valley so dark.

Scientific and Christian Hope, Side by Side

None of the church-based studies I am reporting in this book had to do with hope directly, but one of my former dissertation students, Brian Goetsch, studied the relationship of prayer and hope among Christian college students. Once a day for two weeks students were guided through a prayer exercise or a relaxation exercise on their smartphone. A third group had no intervention, but completed the hope measure at the beginning and end of the study. The study was plagued with various problems—we didn't know how seriously participants engaged in the prayer and relaxation exercises, for example. Did prayer play in the background as the participant studied or watched television, or was it fully engaged as a spiritual discipline? The sample sizes were respectable, but not large. Two weeks isn't very long for any sort of prayer intervention. How different are prayer and relaxation? I could go on and on with limitations.

Figure 5.2
Prayer and Hope

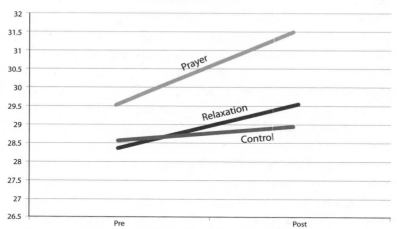

Scores on the State Hope Scale before and after the two-week intervention. Sample sizes were 36 for the prayer group, 35 for the relaxation group, and 39 for the control group.

Still, even with the limitations that plague almost every dissertation project, we found that if we just compared the prayer and the control group, there was a significant change in hope for the prayer group (see figure 5.2). Perhaps this reflects the relational nature of hope. If relationships are promoted through conversation, then talking with God (prayer) should also enhance one's relationship with God. And if hope is relational, then it makes sense that prayer might make a difference.

Redeeming Hope

Learning from Positive Psychology

I've been tough on the positive psychology of hope in this chapter, but remember I think it deserves three and a half stars. For too long psychologists have focused on hopelessness, and I'm glad to see we are now considering the virtue of hope. And the positive psychologists are right that hope takes a degree of vision and tenacity. I think of the widow I described a few pages ago, and the various folks in my Sunday school class suffering from cancer and other afflictions, and they will all do best if they are able to craft a vision for what comes next and then work courageously to get there. It would be nice if the toughest things of life involved buckets of ice water and leg-lift contests, but we all know that is not the case. Life is hard.

The new science of virtue teaches us that those who experience hope amidst life's difficulties will experience health-related benefits, but none of us escapes trouble altogether.

I mentioned earlier in this chapter that Anthony Scioli and his colleagues have suggested an alternative to the pathways/agency model of hope that has dominated the scientific literature. Scioli suggests that hope is multifaceted, involving spirituality and social connection. Because Christian thought brings a relational view of hope, it should encourage social scientists to consider what Scioli has to say and to nudge the direction of our studies toward his model rather than the well-established cognitive model suggested by Snyder and his colleagues.

What Can Christian Thought Offer to Hope?

Model quibbling aside, perhaps the biggest contribution that Christianity can offer to the study of hope is what happens in faith communities all over the world, week after week. I'm not entirely sure why churchgoers live longer than others (a fact rather well established in the demographic literature, though cause and effect is certainly not clear), but I suspect that hope may have something to do with it. I recently heard a colleague say that she received more than forty sympathy cards when her mother passed away. Her brother, not a churchgoer, received two. If Christianity calls us to a relational view of hope fulfilled in knowing Jesus, it also calls us to know one another, to be invested in the lives of our brothers and sisters, to know and be known. Even as Moltmann reminds us that eschatology is hope, present and future, our everyday interactions are examples of sharing our hope, loaning it to others when theirs might be depleted and receiving it from them when ours is running low.

The connection between hardship and hope is seen clearly in Christian teaching, and both point toward the importance of knowing and experiencing relationship with God. In writing to Christ followers in Rome, the apostle Paul makes the connection explicit: "We can rejoice, too, when we run into problems and trials, for we know that they help us develop endurance. And endurance develops strengths of character, and character strengthens our confident hope of salvation. And this hope will not lead to disappointment. For we know how dearly God loves us, because he has given us the Holy Spirit to fill our hearts with his love" (Rom. 5:3–5).

The Church Can Benefit from the Science of Hope

One benefit of science is that it brings implicit experiences into the open places of conversation and inquiry. The science of hope, if taken seriously, may help us study and better understand the role of hope in Christian community.

In 1999, as I walked across the parking lot toward my car from the locked inpatient psychiatric unit where I did psychological evaluations once or twice a week, I had an epiphany that changed my professional life. I remember thinking about the patient I had just interviewed, the report I would be writing late into the evening, how hopeless and isolated she seemed to be, and then recalling how often my reports had a similar paragraph about the patients I had seen. Though we live in a world with constant entertainment and motion, and now more social networking options than we could have imagined in 1999, many people struggle with isolation, and with isolation comes hopelessness. My epiphany started in the form of a question. Where do people find connection in today's society? The answer followed quickly: in faith communities. Faith communities aren't perfect, but they are places where people often experience connection with one another and with God, and in the process they find hope. I committed to turn my professional attention toward the church for however many years I might be granted in this career of mine. This epiphany has changed my research and my clinical work and has redeemed my understanding of hope.

Hope in Christian Counseling

I've been tough on the pathway/agency view of hope in this chapter, in part because it minimizes the relational nature of hope that we see in Christianity. Still, the pathway/agency perspective can be helpful in counseling, especially if offered in the context of a safe and secure relationship, which is what most counseling relationships become over time. A pathway offers a vision forward, though sometimes this seems muddled to clients when they first come for help. Over time, as they begin to sift through their layers of pain and despair, they remember their core values, and perhaps even the virtues that underlie those values. And when this happens, they glimpse the pathway forward. Experienced counselors can tell stories of these transitions: the dark clouds recede and the sun peeks through for a moment in the session, and in this surprising instant there is hope and inspiration and peace. It is a powerful experience for both client and counselor, often accompanied by tears of joy. The clouds will return, of course, and then recede again, perhaps over and over, but the pathway has been set.

Agency involves pain tolerance in counseling, just as it involved pain tolerance of a different kind for Charlie Gibson sticking his hand in that ice water or my daughter in our family leg-lift contest. Too often we counselors forget this and lead our clients to believe that we can somehow help them escape their pain. After decades of doing the work, I'm not so sure about that anymore. Some pain just has to be accepted and endured because it cannot be escaped. But if there is a pathway forward, and a secure relationship has been established, it's amazing to watch the changes that are possible and the hope that motivates the changes.

In Christian counseling, and in the church, our shared faith beliefs can inform both pathway and agency, as well as add the relational support we experience with a loving God. The pathway stretches farther forward for those who believe in the enduring love of God and in the hope of life abundant and eternal. Agency is informed by centuries of believers who have gone before us, enduring various trials and struggles, because the pathway forward required it (see Heb. 11 and 12). And in every pathway we have a companion—one who understands what it is like to suffer and endure enormous hardship—because God was not content to leave us alone in our squalor, but came to us to walk in our midst and show us how to live.

May the church be a place open to studying what we profess, and in the process, may we all be pointed toward hope that transcends human willpower and calls us to know Jesus.

> Now may the God of peace—
> > who brought up from the dead our Lord Jesus,
> the great Shepherd of the sheep,
> > and ratified an eternal covenant with his blood—
> may he equip you with all you need
> > for doing his will.
> May he produce in you,
> > through the power of Jesus Christ,
> every good thing that is pleasing to him.
> > All glory to him forever and ever! Amen.

(Heb. 13:20–21)

6

Grace

When thinking of a virtuous person, most of us imagine a giver. She gives generously of her time and resources, reaching out to colleagues and neighbors in need. He cares deeply about his children and makes personal sacrifices for their welfare. She forgives those who have been unfair and hurtful and acts kindly toward others, even when they are not kind to her. He gives up his desire for public recognition and works hard to make others more virtuous and caring.

In the upside-down economy of Christianity, the core of virtue starts with receiving rather than giving. A virtuous person is first someone who gets something for nothing; it's the "freeloader" who is utterly unable to pay back the monumental gift he or she has received. The more we try to pay it back, the more we resist the gift that is the seed of all virtue. Although Christian virtue ultimately leads to giving and generosity toward others, it begins with the Great Receiving. It begins with grace.

It may seem strange to include a chapter on grace when legitimate questions could be raised about whether it is even a virtue. After all, grace is more a quality of God than of humans, and it never shows up on the classic lists of virtues that have been considered throughout the centuries. I have chosen to include grace for several reasons.

First, most of the virtues are faint human reflections of God's attributes. Though it is true that none of us can be gracious as God is gracious, it seems reasonable to assume that we can experience and express a limited form of grace toward one another, just as we can forgive one another, but never as fully or perfectly as God exemplifies. We can never be as humble as Jesus, or as wise, but still we can aspire toward these qualities. In this sense, grace can be considered a virtue.

Second, it is closely tied to gratitude, which is considered a virtue. When Oprah Winfrey interviewed Elie Wiesel, the Romanian-born Nobel Peace Prize winner and humanitarian, for the November 2000 issue of O: The Oprah Magazine, Wiesel observed: "For me, every hour is grace. And I feel gratitude in my heart each time I can meet someone and look at his or her smile." Gratitude is the proper response—perhaps the only reasonable response—to the gifts of grace that fill creation. I emphasized the word "gift" in the gratitude chapter, and it will also be scattered liberally through this chapter. Some recent biblical scholars see "gift" and "grace" as synonyms.[1]

Third, it seems likely that grace will become increasingly important in positive psychology, which is the contemporary science of virtue. The Templeton Foundation recently funded Project Amazing Grace,[2] and it seems likely additional funding will follow. Some of the leading positive psychologists who study gratitude have become interested in grace, so more good science will be coming our way on this topic.

Fourth, God's grace could be perceived as the hub of all other virtues. Without glimpsing God's grace or experiencing God's common grace, which affects all creation whether we acknowledge it or not, would it even be possible for us to forgive one another? What would hope look like if not for the justifying, sanctifying, and glorifying grace of God? Can we even picture wisdom without the gift of God's gracious presence in our lives and our world? Gifts make us grateful, or they should, which is why gratitude is so closely linked to grace. Humility—the ability to see beyond myself and focus on the other—is possible because this is true of God's gracious character, made crystal clear in the incarnation, life, death, and resurrection of Jesus. Even faith—long considered to be a Christian virtue—is only possible because of God's grace (Eph. 2:8–9).

Fifth, though this book is not primarily about counseling, I have attempted to make connections to counseling in each chapter. As a clinical psychologist, I have long felt that counseling and psychotherapy are, at least to some extent, an exercise in grace. Ever since reading Frederick Buechner's book *A Place Called Remember*,[3] I have been drawn to Norman Rockwell's painting titled *Saying Grace*. Buechner described the painting so powerfully in his book that I felt compelled to find and order a copy to hang in our dining room. In the painting an old woman and a young boy—presumably the woman's grandson—sit in a crowded, smoke-filled restaurant and bow to say grace before eating. Two teenagers across the table, one with a cigarette dangling from his mouth, lean in to get a closer look at what is happening. This picture, it seems to me, is not so much about praying before a meal as it is about being messengers of grace in a noisy, complicated, messy world. That's what counseling is: sitting with people in the complicated places of life, with such a calm and gracious presence that it makes people want to lean in and get a closer look.

Finally, it is personally important to me because I have spent my entire adult life pondering grace.[4] I certainly don't have it figured out and probably never will this side of heaven, but I love to stare at grace, to study its nuances, contours, and meaning, to consider how it can seep into my life and guide the way I relate to God and others. If I can sneak a chapter on grace into this book on virtue, then it gives me one more opportunity to saturate my heart and mind with the most important topic I can imagine.

SIDEBAR 6.1

Dimensions of Grace

The Dimensions of Grace Scale is a thirty-six-item scale that combines items from earlier scales. Using a statistical procedure called factor analysis, the authors were able to identify five subscales. Here are the subscales and sample items from each.

Experiencing God's Grace

"God is in the process of making me more like Jesus."

Costly Grace (related to Bonhoeffer's notion of "cheap grace")

"My behavior does not matter since I've been forgiven."

Grace to Self

"I seldom feel shame."

Grace from Others

"As a child I was confident that at least one of my parents loved me no matter what."

Grace to Others

"When offended or harmed by others I generally find it easy to forgive them."

The Science of Grace

Social scientists distinguish between theoretical and empirical research, with the former being articles that advance our conceptual understanding of a topic and the latter involving data collection and analysis. Because positive psychology has become such a dominant force in the social sciences over the past twenty years, most of the topics studied in this book have a robust empirical literature showing how a particular virtue is good for individual and relational health. Grace is an exception. There are some theoretical articles in the scientific literature, but few empirical articles.

Preliminary evidence suggests that emphasizing grace with couples results in increased empathy, forgiveness, and reconciliation.[5]

We also have some initial evidence suggesting a grace orientation is related to decreased levels of depression and anxiety and increased general mental health.[6] We know that Christian leaders would like psychologists to better understand a Christian doctrine of sin and all of its implications for grace, because without sin we cannot fully understand grace.[7] Other than these few articles, most empirical studies of grace have focused on scale development, with a relatively recent scale—the Dimensions of Grace Scale—combining items from three earlier scales.[8]

Though we don't have much empirical evidence regarding grace, key scientists are poised to do more research on the topic, and at least one major foundation is interested in funding research in the area, so it seems likely that more science will appear soon. Here are the sorts of questions that Project Amazing Grace would like to see addressed in future research.

1. How is grace learned?
2. Why is it so difficult to accept the idea of grace?
3. How does grace transform us?
4. How does grace help us to grow, spiritually and emotionally?
5. To what extent does grace help to shield us from negative emotional experiences such as loneliness and shame?
6. To what extent does grace enhance mental health outcomes such as joy and contentment?
7. What is the link between seeing ourselves as broken and accepting grace from God?
8. Do our views and experiences of grace change the likelihood of offering grace to others?
9. Is grace connected to humility and self-forgiveness?
10. How does grace impact the work of counseling and psychotherapy?
11. How might a science of grace impact the church?
12. How can grace be taught?

13. What are common misuses and problems with our under-
    standing of grace?
14. Might it harm people to give them something they don't
    deserve? If so, how does this affect our understanding of
    grace?

Clearly, there is much work to be done on this topic. A vibrant
positive psychology of grace might help build bridges between
scientific and faith communities, and help us understand some
of the benefits experienced for those aware of the gift of grace.

Moving toward a Christian View of Grace

However much we may unpack the mysteries of grace, we will
never know it completely, and certainly not with science. Christian
author and psychologist Alan Tjeltveit points out that "neither
God nor grace can be fully (and perhaps not even partially) quantified and manipulated," as science requires.[9] Grace, this unfathomable gift from God, reflects the character of the Creator, who,
paradoxically, both wants to be known and is too far above the
created order to be fully known by finite mortals. So perhaps the
first contribution of a Christian view of grace is to point out that
grace is impossible to fully apprehend.

Early in my career I wrote a book about grace, which I tried du-
tifully to get published by sending it around to various publishers.
It never got published, and now I am grateful for that. A couple
decades later I published two books about grace, and while I'm
mostly pleased with these later books, there are several things I
got wrong—probably more than I know.[10] No matter how deeply
we study the topic of grace, we can never fully comprehend it.
Grace, like God's character itself, is too vast to grasp, describe,
or contain.

Another contribution of Christianity is to remind us how countercultural the notion of grace is, which may be one reason it is so

difficult to grasp. The notion of self-sufficiency is celebrated in contemporary life. I live in a state that has Self-Sufficiency Offices run
by the Department of Human Services, which is quite the paradox
because the purpose of the offices is to provide food, cash, child
care, and refugee assistance for those in need. But none of us wants
to be in need, so we will be more likely to go to the Self-Sufficiency
Office than to the I Need Help Office. It's easy to find online guides
for self-sufficient living, and there is even a *Self Sufficiency Magazine*, with the tagline "Ideas for Living a Self Sufficient Lifestyle."
And, if I'm honest, I have to admit that I'm a fan of all of these.
It delights me to know that Oregon has offices to help those in
need and that they also have goals to help needy families and individuals move toward financial independence. The self-sufficiency
websites tell people how to raise chickens and save water and keep
their own bees, and the magazine gives ideas for how to preserve
food, grow great potatoes, and all sorts of other creative home-
steading ideas. I grow potatoes and raise chickens and honeybees,
I help Lisa preserve food whenever I can find the time, and I own
five ladders because it is emotionally easier to buy another ladder
than to ask a neighbor to lend me one. I could be a showpiece for
self-sufficiency.

Jesus invites me, and self-sufficient people like me, to be needy.
As much as I resist the invitation, it is the only pathway to grace.
Accepting God's invitation to be needy takes the focus off me
and puts it on the gift and its giver. In a psalm that I have read
hundreds of times in my life, Israel's King David concludes with
these words: "As for me, since I am poor and needy, let the Lord
keep me in his thoughts. You are my helper and my savior. O my
God, do not delay" (Ps. 40:17). David understood struggle and
failure, and he understood grace.

Not only do we live in a time when self-sufficiency is glamor-
ized, but we also have lost the language of sin.[11] I wrote of sin in
the previous chapter, so I won't linger here, but if we neglect a
theology of sin, we simultaneously cheapen our understanding
of grace. Grace becomes leniency, or just being nice.

Sometimes students ask me for grace in turning in a paper an hour or a day late or a week late. Depending on the circumstances, I may say yes or no, but I always tell them that this is not grace. They are simply asking for kindness and compassion, which I like to offer them whenever it feels responsible to do so, but all the kindness in the world will never sum to grace.

Grace is a gift to one who not only does not deserve a thing but can never possibly deserve or earn it. It is a terrifying reality to be in a place where grace is appealing, like being stranded at night in a foreign country where you don't know the language, or along a desert highway with a dead cell phone and no water. And in this place of desperation, when any hope of self-sufficiency is fully expired, we begin to understand how much we long for the gift of grace, because it is the gift of life itself.

Like the apostle Paul, blinded by truth on the Damascus Road, we have our world shaken by grace and are forced to look beyond our own zeal and dedication to whatever it is we may deem important. Grace turns everything upside down and inside out and forces us to acknowledge how poor and needy we truly are.

Patience is another contribution that Christianity offers to the study of grace. Science tends to be time limited, looking at change over a few weeks or months. If a follow-up measurement is done at all, it tends to be after an additional few weeks or months. But grace, oh, it is a lifelong pursuit that requires incredible patience. If John Newton, author of "Amazing Grace," had completed his self-report posttests a year or two after his eighteenth-century conversion on the turbulent seas of the Atlantic, he would have likely shown certain changes in terms of his understanding of virtue and faith, but he would have been filling out the surveys while he was captaining a slave ship. We tend to tell the story without much nuance—that Newton was a slave trader, had a conversion experience, became a pastor, wrote "Amazing Grace," and fought for the abolition of slavery. That's all true, but we tend not to mention that he traded slaves for nearly ten years after his conversion and that he stopped only because of a medical problem. He once wrote in his journal that slave trading was an optimal life for a Christian because it afforded him time to study Scripture on the long trips across the Atlantic.[12]

But grace didn't stop its work with Newton's conversion, and it doesn't stop for modern-day Christians either. Grace keeps going, the gift keeps on giving, doing its sanctifying work, sometimes over a long period of time. Eventually Newton studied theology, began pastoring, and became profoundly convicted of his sin. A friend would later say that he never spent thirty minutes with Newton during which his remorse for slave trading didn't come up. And Newton did fight for abolition, but only after grace awakened him to the evil of slavery. On his deathbed he noted that his memory was failing, but that he remembered two things clearly: that he was a great sinner, and Christ was a great savior.

Amazing, grace is. But sometimes it takes years for us to see just how amazing it is.

We Christians sometimes think of grace as a one-time event that points us toward heaven and erases our sins, and when we do this we neglect the ongoing, life-giving power of sanctifying grace. It changes us over a lifetime more than it changes us over days or weeks or months.

Grace's Telos

Throughout these chapters on virtue I have attempted to envision what each virtue might look like in the fully functioning person. This is challenging because we live in a time when telos is not much considered. We're more likely to ask, "Why should I have to change?" than to ask, "What would I be like as a whole and healthy person?"

It is tempting to discuss grace and telos based on the sort of generous, helpful people we become as a result of God's grace. This is true enough, but I fear moving too quickly to the ways we reflect grace toward others cheapens the conversation about grace. Receiving God's grace is at the center of wholeness.

Theologian John Barclay points toward the fullness of grace in six dimensions. First, it is *superabundant*, supreme and lavish in its scope.[13] Metaphors fail to capture how large the gift of grace truly is, but the closer we get to understanding its magnitude, the more our moments are filled with gratitude and hope, forgiveness and wisdom and humility. Second is the *singularity* of the gift. God's intention is not mixed, and there is no secondary gain here. God's gift is offered in pure, singular benevolence. Third, the *priority* of timing is essential. The gift is offered before any initiative on our part. We do not earn or deserve grace. Grace comes first. Fourth is the *incongruity* of the gift. The magnitude of grace makes no sense in an economic mind-set that equates the value of a gift with the worth of the receiver. Fifth, and central to the concept of telos, is the *efficacy* of the gift. Grace changes us, seeping deep into our character. Sixth, grace is *noncircular*. It's not like when I give a gift to you because you always give a gift to me every Christmas, and you give a gift to me because I always give a gift to you. No, grace escapes reciprocity and is offered unilaterally by God to humanity.

Because of the efficacy of the gift, we are changed by grace. We reflect the gift, however dimly, in our interactions with others. Science will never help us figure out the character of God, who offers such an amazing gift, but it can help us figure out at least some of its efficacy. How does grace change us, and what implications does it have for our living alongside one another?

Science and Grace, Side by Side

Two of the projects funded by the Templeton Foundation grant I have described throughout this book considered grace and its implications for human functioning. The projects shared similar methodologies, but the results were quite distinct.

Jeff Moody, a doctoral student working under the supervision of Rodger Bufford, looked at the effects of a grace campaign in two moderate-sized congregations.[14] Specifically, Jeff wondered whether marriage might provide an ideal context to practice grace with one another, thereby enhancing the marriage relationship. As was true in all the projects funded by this grant, the pastors of the respective churches were highly involved in the process. They worked with Jeff to identify a strategy for a grace campaign in each congregation. The campaign involved a six-week sermon series, small groups meeting to discuss James Bryan Smith's book *The Good and Beautiful God*, and a variety of grace practices that were provided to congregants each week by email and hard copy.[15] Married couples were encouraged to work on the practices together. Approximately thirty individuals from each congregation completed a set of questionnaires, and then Congregation 1 engaged in the grace campaign. After six weeks the same thirty individuals from both congregations completed the questionnaires again, then Congregation 1 went back to ministry as usual while Congregation 2 engaged in the grace campaign. At the end of Congregation 2's campaign, the same folks completed questionnaires again. Jeff expected marital satisfaction to increase in Congregation 1 during the first time period, and to increase in Congregation 2 during the second time period.

As is true of much science, Jeff didn't find what he expected, but he found something else. Married participants didn't respond any differently than unmarried participants. However, changes in the Dimensions of Grace Scale (see sidebar 6.1 on p. 144) corresponded to the grace campaigns. As expected, grace increased in Congregation 1, but not in Congregation 2, during the first phase of the study. At first glance this may seem like a statement of the obvious: a grace campaign heightens people's awareness of grace. But it also provides some important affirmation for an emerging measurement tool used to assess people's experience of grace.

Laura Geczy-Haskins conducted the second study under my supervision.[16] Laura used a design similar to Jeff's, but with two smaller congregations, and with nine-week grace campaigns instead of six-week campaigns. She was particularly interested in self-forgiveness. Does a ministry emphasis on grace affect people's ability and willingness to forgive themselves for past wrongs?

Self-forgiveness is a tricky thing to measure because it can be so easily confused with self-excusing. For example, imagine that I do or say something harmful, or even hateful, to my spouse. I could deal with the dissonance this causes me by convincing myself that she deserves it or that it wasn't that big a deal. If so, I am merely excusing myself and not actually forgiving myself. True self-forgiveness involves recognizing the damage I have caused, experiencing responsibility and remorse for it, and then choosing to forgive myself and move forward in life. Laura and I came up with this table to help distinguish true self-forgiveness from pseudo-self-forgiveness.

		Release from Self-Recrimination	
		Low	High
Responsibility for Harm	Low	Unawareness	Pseudo-self-forgiveness
	High	Self-condemnation	Genuine self-forgiveness

In order to measure true self-forgiveness, Laura assessed both the extent of responsibility people reported for a past misdeed and the extent to which they had forgiven themselves. She used several different self-forgiveness scales, including those that measure the state and trait of self-forgiveness. As discussed in previous chapters, state measures look at a specific instance, and trait measures look at general tendencies. Trait self-forgiveness has also been called self-forgivingness.

The trait forgiveness findings turned out just as Laura expected (see figure 6.1). Congregation 1 increased in trait self-forgiveness during their grace campaign and then plateaued when going

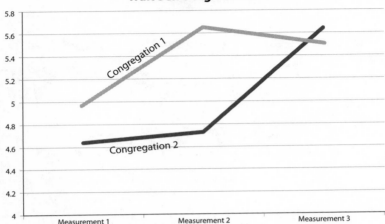

Figure 6.1
Trait Self-Forgiveness

Trait self-forgiveness was measured with the self-forgiveness items on the Heartland Forgiveness Scale. Notice that trait self-forgiveness increased in Congregation 1 throughout their grace campaign, and then in Congregation 2 when they engaged in the grace campaign. See Laura Yamhure Thompson et al., "Dispositional Forgiveness of Self, Others, and Situations," *Journal of Personality* 73 (2005): 313–60.

back to ministry as usual. Congregation 2 increased in trait self-forgiveness during their grace campaign. Her findings on the state self-forgiveness scales were not as compelling, in part because we made the mistake of having participants imagine a specific offense each time they took the questionnaires without ensuring that they were imagining the same offense each time. Still, even with this methodological oversight, we did see an overall increase in state self-forgiveness over time for both congregations, though it was not linked to the specific timing of the grace campaigns, as was trait self-forgiveness. No changes were seen in the responsibility-for-offense measure we used, so we can be relatively confident that the increases in self-forgiveness and self-forgivingness were not just an artifact of self-excusing.

Though it was not a hypothesized finding, it is interesting that Laura also found a change in intrinsic religiousness associated with the grace campaigns (see figure 6.2). Intrinsic religion is marked

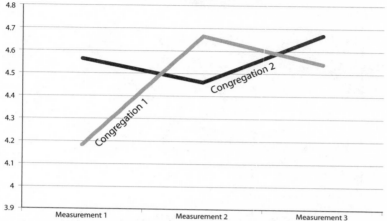

Figure 6.2
Intrinsic Religiousness

Intrinsic religiousness was measured with the Duke Religion Index. Intrinsic religiousness increased in Congregation 1 during their grace campaign, and not in Congregation 2. Intrinsic religiousness turned upward in Congregation 2 during their grace campaign. The results are complicated by the differences in congregations before the study began. See Harold Koenig and Arndt Büssing, "The Duke University Religion Index (DUREL): A Five-Item Measure for Use in Epidemiological Studies," *Religions* 1 (2010): 78–85.

by personal commitment to the beliefs of a religion and also by efforts to live consistently with those beliefs. The grace campaigns corresponded with increases in intrinsic religion in each of the congregations, though the findings are complicated by the fact that the two congregations differed in intrinsic religiousness before the study even began. Still, it seems likely that grace makes us more consistent in our beliefs and behaviors. These relationships between grace and fidelity to religious beliefs and values are worth studying more, as grace becomes the focus of increased scientific inquiry.

Redeeming Grace

Learning from Positive Psychology

At this point positive psychology doesn't have much to offer to the study of grace, though it may soon. We have some preliminary ways to measure people's experience of grace, and some initial evidence that emphasizing grace enhances individual and relational mental health. It also seems clear that focusing on grace promotes self-forgiveness, and from this we might surmise that it is also likely to increase interpersonal forgiveness. Beyond this, we have many intriguing scientific questions to pursue and growing curiosity about grace in the scientific community. The best science on grace is yet to come.

What Can Christian Thought Offer to Grace?

In contrast to the limited contributions that science can offer to the study of grace, Christian thought is replete with resources on grace. Indeed, it is difficult to even imagine a science of grace without the foundation of Christian thought. I mention only four contributions from Christian thought here, but many more could be described. Each of the four I have selected has implications for the conversation between science and faith.

First, a Christian doctrine of grace is foundational to how we understand a person. Grace shapes how we understand what goes wrong with people and what goes right. Through grace, we find the God-given courage to admit our finitude and sinfulness, and through grace we are redeemed and sanctified, called to a new and abundant life. As the science continues to grow, it will be interesting to see how a Christian view of persons, including beliefs about sin and grace, plays out with regard to psychological health. Some years ago Lisa and I embarked on an ambitious scale-development project to measure people's beliefs about sin and grace. We collected data from hundreds and hundreds of people, but never published our findings. What I recall from our fledgling efforts to measure these huge theological constructs is that believing oneself to be a sinner does not at all predispose one to be depressed or psychologically troubled. This finding would likely surprise some nonreligious social scientists who see Christian anthropology as an oppressive way of perceiving oneself.

Second, grace transforms how we make meaning and live into our beliefs, and this is a natural area for scientific exploration. Though science may never be able to explore the essence or meaning of grace itself, it can certainly look at the life implications for one who experiences grace.[17] Those who experience grace most profoundly might be expected to show certain measurable benefits with regard to death anxiety, happiness, forgiveness, gratitude, hope, and more.

Third, understanding grace requires one to be immersed in a life of forgiveness. I can understand a Christian view of grace only if I believe myself to be in need of and a recipient of God's forgiveness. As the magnitude of God's gift begins to seep around the edges of my defensiveness, it is only reasonable that I offer forgiveness to others as well in response. We have already discussed, in chapter 2, the impressive body of research showing the benefits of interpersonal forgiveness. I hope a science of grace will consider the complex relationships between how one experiences grace, the extent to which one forgives others and perceives forgiveness from God, and the related physical, emotional, spiritual, and relational benefits.

Fourth, grace frees us from self-focus and allows us to experience love of God and neighbor. A Christian view of grace shatters any image that I can earn my way, be good enough to garner God's attention and love. In this, it should also allow me a deep and true freedom—not the sort of freedom that pronounces I have the right to do anything I may choose to do, but the sort of freedom that releases me from the prison of self-obsession and allows me to see the world around me. In the humility chapter (chap. 4) I discussed Anthony Hoekema's notion that being made in the image of God means reclaiming connections with God, other, and nature, as well as being in a harmonious relationship with self.[18] Hoekema's schema is an optimal picture of freedom. Grace means that I can turn my eyes outward to notice the smile of a friend, the majesty of a rolling ocean wave, the goodness of God revealed in the morning dew and springtime green, the simple beauty of good food, and the deep peace found in corporate worship.

Of course, many more resources from Christian thought could be offered to the positive psychology of grace. These four are intended as conversation starters rather than as an exhaustive list of how Christianity can inform a science of grace.

The Church Can Benefit from the Science of Grace

We Christians have a choice to make. One option is to hold on tight to concepts such as forgiveness, gratitude, hope, and grace—to shake our fists at the scientists and declare that these constructs have always been ours and that scientists have no right to take them away. In one sense, this might be a reasonable response. After all, science has taken these religious ideas, built measurement strategies to quantify them, and then exported them into the secular world as if they require no religious or philosophical moorings.

Still, we have another option. Rather than resentfully clinging to these religious virtues, we can celebrate the attention they are getting outside the walls of our churches. Conversations about forgiveness are now prominent in popular books and magazines as well as in counseling and health-care settings. So are topics such as gratitude and hope, and someday grace may be also. And while it's true that these constructs may be slightly anemic when taken outside a Christian context, we can delight in their ubiquity and even see them as invitations for those outside the church to come into the church, where they can explore these ideas more.

This is our choice. We can see science as the competition and even resent it for taking away our cherished virtues, or we can partner together and find ways to help make the science better. And, in turn, maybe the science of virtue will help make the church better by bringing the virtues we care about most into mainstream conversation.

Grace in Christian Counseling

As I suggested at the beginning of this chapter, I see counseling as an exercise in grace, however dimly we may reflect God's immense grace toward us. Consider two ways this may play out in the practical, everyday work of counselors.

First, most counselors have clients they don't naturally enjoy or like. I recall seeing a man for anger problems because his employer insisted he get therapy or get fired. He was a great salesman but a difficult person to be around. He screamed at coworkers in the hallway and made the workplace toxic for many. Honestly, he had a similar impact on me. I dreaded the hour every week, at least for the first six weeks of our work together. But then I remembered that when I find a client distasteful, it's often a lack of empathy on my part, so I redoubled my efforts to hear his stories, to kindle grace in my own soul rather than defensiveness and anger. When he treated me rudely, I leaned even more into kindness, and to my surprise his angry, brittle defenses began to break down. With time, he began to open up and tell me stories of past vulnerability, such as what it was like to be a frightened little boy banished outside his family's trailer during a cold Indiana winter morning because he had wet his bed. There he sat, shivering in wet underwear, determining that he would never again lose control of anything in his life. He had other stories too, but this is the one that sticks with me most clearly and the one that helped me to understand his demeanor with his work colleagues and with me. My client learned early that either he was in full control or he was exiled. Given those choices, no wonder he chose control, time after time.

Grace leans into merciful kindness, even when a person appears to be annoying and undeserving. For the Christian counselor, this is a theological commitment as much as a counseling strategy, because each of us has received immense grace from God, though we have no way to earn or deserve it.

When we were utterly helpless, Christ came at just the right time and died for us sinners. Now, most people would not be willing to die for an upright person, though someone might perhaps be willing to die for a person who is especially good. But God showed his great love for us by sending Christ to die for us while we were still sinners. And since we have been made right in God's sight by the blood of Christ, he will certainly save us from God's condemnation. For since our friendship with God was restored by the death of his Son while we were still his enemies, we will certainly be saved through the life of his Son. So now we can rejoice in our wonderful new relationship with God because our Lord Jesus Christ has made us friends of God. (Rom. 5:6–11)

From this center of divine grace, we offer some semblance of grace to those who need someone to listen and care. Grace creates a space so safe that pain, abuse, and failure can be confronted, a space typically accompanied by words that every effective counselor hears over and over: "I've never told anyone that story before."

Second, grace persists. Sometimes we Christians get the idea that grace redeems us once, perhaps when we're sitting around a bonfire at a summer camp, and then we're on our own to grow into a mature, virtuous person who loves God and neighbor. We cheapen grace when we think such a thing, because grace is a persistent, sanctifying, ever-present force that conforms us more and more to the image of Jesus long after the bonfire embers fade. Grace calls us farther in, higher up, to places where our passions are ordered and love flows naturally from our character, transformed over years of a long obedience. And this has implications for Christian counseling.

For one, it reminds us as Christian counselors that even as we journey with our clients, we are also on our own journey. God is working in us and through us, calling us in grace to remain tender and compassionate amidst the stress of our work, to live into the virtue of Jesus. Also, it reminds us that God is active with our clients. The change we see over ten or twenty weeks of counseling is important, but it's not exhaustive, and it's not all up to us. God's grace persists, long after people leave our offices and return to their day-to-day lives. They may struggle again with depression and sour relationships and anxiety and addiction, or they may not, but however mysterious and counterintuitive it may seem, God's grace persists through it all. Perhaps one of the most important things we can do as counselors is to see grace everywhere and to invite our clients to do the same.

■ ■ ■ ■ ■

My oldest granddaughter was born in 2010 after my daughter endured quite a tough labor. While Lisa was away with Megan Anna and Luke at the hospital, I was anxiously pacing our little farm, about thirty miles away, pondering what life would be like as a grandparent. When Grace Auden was finally born and named, I happily reconstructed some lyrics to an old hymn and sang these words to her many times over her first year of life.

> Grace, Grace, God's Grace
> Grace to flourish and Grace to be free.
> Grace, Grace, God's Grace
> Grace so precious, so dear to me.

Holding little Grace Auden in a rocking chair, singing these words to a grandchild who could do nothing to deserve my love and can never do anything to lose it—I can get no closer than that to understanding God's grace toward me and all creation. It is the Great Receiving, the gift, the beginning of Christian virtue.

Conclusion

Let's Work Together

Excited about beginning the final chapter of this book, I put my laptop in my backpack and headed out on a short walk to one of my favorite lunch places and about the only place in my small town that still has a salad bar. After ordering my mini pizza and crafting my spinach salad, replete with all sorts of healthy veggies and some not-so-healthy dressing, I sat down at the table, opened my laptop, and mindlessly reached for the saltshaker to season my salad.

It must be the oldest prank in the book of pranks, but it had never happened to me in my fifty-eight years of living. Instead of a few granules coming out, the entire contents of the saltshaker dumped onto my salad—a small mountain of white atop my spinach leaves. I imagined how some previous customer might laugh in delight seeing the old professor scraping salt out of his spinach salad. After too many bites, each one exceeding my daily recommended sodium allowance, I determined the salad to be inedible and sheepishly approached the counter for a fresh start. The employee handled it gracefully, offering me a clean bowl and condolences.

And so I sat, pondering the final chapter in a book on virtue while being surrounded with the slurry of complexity that we call contemporary life. One person removes the lid of a saltshaker, not so much out of malice or spite, but just to be funny. It ends up costing the restaurant and a customer, but hey, it's funny. Another person tries to eat an overly salted salad, not wanting to inconvenience the restaurant, but eventually determines that he can't endure the layers of salt coating every veggie and leaf of spinach, and so decides to ask for the favor of another salad. A third person hears yet another customer complaint and responds with kindness. Here, in the pizza restaurant, we see the swirl of virtue and self-centeredness that makes up daily life.

Distracted by the salty salad, instead of writing I found myself reading a news article about big data. The article is about a book by a mathematician with a PhD from Harvard exploring how "weapons of math destruction" are being used to discriminate against underprivileged citizens when it comes to employment, jail sentencing, and mortgage rates. People who live in certain neighborhoods, often those with high proportions of people of color, are expected to pay higher mortgage rates or are given longer jail or prison sentences because of the algorithms used to determine risk. With every paragraph I felt more troubled and appalled.

This is the world that Jesus enters, walking in the midst of all our muddled motives and intentions, seeing both our self-centeredness and decency, embodying truth and grace, and showing us how to live. And then Jesus commissioned the church to carry on, to keep demonstrating what an abundant life looks like in our broken world, where unpredictable saltshakers are among the very least of our concerns.

The church can be an enclave of virtue, and in many ways it should be, but it also can move outward into the messy world, as Jesus did. The call I have offered here, for the church to engage with science, is an invitation for the church to do the difficult work of mingling with contemporary culture. We are, Jesus says, the salt of the earth.

Visioning the Possibilities

The church and psychology have sometimes been competitors, but we now face exciting opportunities for collaboration. This goes in two directions, as I have suggested throughout this book.

First, the church can help the science of positive psychology. In many ways, it already has helped by providing many of the leading positive psychology scholars. It's striking how many of the leading scientists in the positive psychology movement are also committed followers of Jesus. The church can also contribute by providing a metaphysic for positive psychology. Why is gratitude worthwhile? What about forgiveness makes it good? In what ways might humility promote a better way of living than self-interest does? These are matters considered by Christians for many centuries, which means the church has an important voice to offer to the science of positive psychology.

Left on its own, positive psychology tends to settle back to a place of self-interest. I forgive because it's good for me. I practice gratitude because it lowers my blood pressure. I pursue hope because it adds to my quality of life. Me, me, me. It's all about The Big Me.[1] Many scientists fail to see the paradox of how a science of virtue can be twisted to be so very self-centered. And to this, the church offers a nudge toward the love of God and neighbor that we have considered throughout this book.

But also at the heart of this book is the assumption that positive psychology can help the church. As society waxes in its trust of science and wanes in its view of religion, positive psychology can contribute to church communities, providing a place for meaningful dialogue where science and faith enhance and sharpen each other.

I have mentioned the Templeton Foundation throughout this book, including grateful references to the grant they provided for studies described in several chapters. At the heart of the Human Sciences division of the Templeton Foundation—and one of Sir John Templeton's driving passions throughout his adult life—is the idea of a humble theology. Sometimes we act as if faith provides the final answers in life and that no further questioning or investigation is needed. This is neither good theology nor good thinking. Faith requires interpretation, and the lenses through which we interpret faith are always influenced by personal and cultural factors. Good theology—theology being sometimes called the queen of sciences—is premised on the assumption that mining the depths of faith is an ongoing dynamic process. We do not have all the final answers, but instead we have a God who longs to be known and who invites us into the mysteries and meanings of life. This is a humble posture, one that calls us to curiosity and hard work, rather than simply declaring to the world that we have everything figured out.

We Christians can resist science, standing defensively while looking for ways it contradicts or challenges our faith, or we can welcome science as a way to grow in humility. When science causes us to question our doctrines and presuppositions, then we are called into the adventure of working harder to understand the apparent inconsistencies and contradictions.

Thankfully, sometimes science and faith will point in similar directions, as seems to be happening now with the study of virtue. This opens new possibilities for collaboration.

What Is the Good Life?

Positive psychology, the church, and Christian counselors can be partners in helping people redefine the good life, but first we have to be clear about it ourselves.

The message we often hear in contemporary society is this: if you aren't happy, change your life to find happiness again. Get a new job, get out of that troubling marriage, try the latest medication being peddled on primetime television, get into therapy, do whatever you have to do to find happiness again. This is what author Russ Harris calls *The Happiness Trap*.[2] We can pursue a sort of happiness that involves pleasure, gratification, and immediate gladness, but in the process we often end up like a caged mouse running around and around on that wheel, always pursuing something that's fleeting. The alternative is to face into our present experiences, even the unpleasant ones, and to seek a life filled with purpose and meaning. We can pursue feeling good, and it probably won't work, or we can pursue living well.

I wonder whether we sometimes succumb to the same trap in American Christianity. We bring our troubles to God, too often assuming that God's primary desire is to remove our suffering and make us happy. But what if God has a different sort of happiness in mind for us—one that calls us to virtue-based living? The apostle Paul, someone familiar with suffering, wrote about this in his letter to Christians scattered throughout Rome: "We can rejoice, too, when we run into problems and trials, for we know that they help us develop endurance. And endurance develops strength of character, and character strengthens our confident hope of salvation. And this hope will not lead to disappointment. For we know how dearly God loves us, because he has given us the Holy Spirit to fill our hearts with his love" (Rom. 5:3–5). If we spend our efforts avoiding pain, it catches up with us anyway, but if we accept pain, we have the choice of not letting it be our boss. Even amidst suffering we see God doing good work and pointing us toward a life of hope, faith, and love—the Christian virtues.

Positive psychology and the church could be partners in promoting a new understanding of the good life in contemporary society, one that focuses more on virtue than pleasure, more on being good than on feeling good. How's that for an ambitious agenda?

A New Frontier for Christian Counseling

Most of the Christian counseling examples throughout this book have been informed by my attraction to a relatively new form of therapy called Acceptance and Commitment Therapy (ACT, pronounced as a single word). Several others have also been interested in exploring ACT from a Christian perspective.[3] The essence of ACT involves accepting life's challenges rather than avoiding them and then committing to one's guiding values in life. I take this even a step further and suggest that virtues may inform our guiding values.

Discussing values in counseling is important, reminding us and our clients of what is important in life and how to live consistently with our values. Virtue goes beyond values and presses us toward who we are becoming. Philosopher Alasdair MacIntyre argues that both Enlightenment philosophy and the Protestant Reformation have made it difficult to imagine a pathway between who a person is and who the person is to become.[4] For example, I may have a value to be loving toward my spouse, and this is a good thing, but in contemporary society I am unlikely to consider the underlying virtue—that marriage is shaping me and helping me to move closer to understanding and living out the fullness of love. As a result, virtue has been reduced to a mere understanding of who we currently are. In other words, we have come to equate virtue with values. If we are to love, to forgive, or to be grateful, it's not so much about realizing some essential dimension of full humanity, but more about a self-defined value to become as healthy and free as one can be.

A full-bodied understanding of virtue calls us toward teleology, toward sanctification, toward understanding we are on a pathway toward becoming more fully the people we were created to be. Imagine how this might look in counseling, if we were able to move beyond the suffering our clients experience, and even beyond helping them live into the values they hold in life, and allow them to imagine the possibilities for who they are becoming. In a Christian counseling context these virtues would undoubtedly be shaped by the church and would include the topics discussed in this book—forgivingness and hope and gratitude, wisdom and humility and grace. Understanding the science associated with each of these topics might, in turn, help counselors consider the mechanisms of change in their clients' lives.

Grieving the Quantified World

Before finishing this book, I must mention one nagging concern. I have felt this concern in writing each chapter, as I suspect many readers will. And I felt it in the pizza restaurant as I read about "weapons of math destruction."

Our world has become highly quantified, and likely too quantified. If I buy movie tickets online today, I will get an email tomorrow asking me to rate the movie I watched so that one more rating can go into someone's relational database along with my demographics and other movie choices. This, in turn, dictates what pop-up advertisements you get on your web browser, at least if you share any of my demographics. Every mouse click is a vote, every purchase at a grocery store, every dollar given to charity. And now, even the virtues we discuss in church are being studied in the ivory tower, quantified with self-report measures and published in scientific journals linked to services that count the number of citations associated with each article, so that authors can be promoted and tenured.

Though I love science, and we quantify almost everything in science, I also feel disquieted by the seeming assumption that the biggest questions and quandaries of life can somehow be coded numerically, analyzed with probabilistic algorithms, and stored in a database. It reminds me of the words of a wise psychologist colleague, Alan Tjeltveit:

> To insist upon reliably measuring all variables before developing an understanding of human beings would, however, require the exclusion from psychology of some "variables" Christians think essential in understanding human beings. We think God exists and actively works in human lives, through the Sacraments, when the Word is preached, and in other ways. Grace is a reality at the heart of the lives of Christians. Neither God nor grace can be fully (and perhaps not even partially) quantified and manipulated, however. And so the scientists' marvelously productive and important methods fall short of addressing some psychological dimensions of

human lives; those methods alone cannot produce a *comprehensive* understanding of human beings.[5]

If you have read this book with some cynicism toward science, I cannot offer complete reassurance. Science cannot plumb the depth of godliness or explore all nuance of virtuous living. But neither is science completely irrelevant or misinformed; it has risen to supremacy in contemporary culture because of its explanatory power, its capacity to extend our life span, and the insight it lends into some of the deepest mysteries of the cosmos. Whether considering the smallest particles of matter or the largest galaxies, science has informed the way we look at all creation.

Rather than embracing all science, or rejecting it all, perhaps the best tactic for Christians is to approach science with critical appreciation. That is, we see its limits and critique the overgeneralizations and excessive confidence it engenders, but we also see its value and appreciate how it allows us to understand creation more fully. This has been my effort throughout this book, to look at positive psychology through a lens of critical appreciation.

Redeeming Virtue

In concluding this brief book, I return to the four dimensions of redeeming virtue that I proposed in the introduction and considered in each of the chapters. First, positive psychology helps us reclaim the language of virtue—a language that has been mostly lost in contemporary times. I am grateful to the men and women who study forgiveness and gratitude and humility and report their findings to the scientific world. Many of these scholars are my friends, and I consider their work to be tremendously important in resurrecting conversations about virtue. Everett Worthington, a gentle and humble man, and one of the world's leading experts on forgiveness and humility, inspires me by his example. He understands forgiveness academically, but also personally, as he has forgiven the killer of his mother. Julie Exline, a scholar who has studied and written widely about many of the virtues discussed in this book, has also spent years learning about spiritual formation. Bob Emmons, who has led the way on gratitude research and is now moving into grace research, coached his son's Little League team and shows remarkable balance in life. Each of these scientists, and many more I could name, are helping reclaim the lost language of virtue, bringing it back into the light after decades (or centuries) of darkness. And they are not alone, as many philosophers and theologians in recent decades have also helped reclaim the language of virtue.

Second, if we in the church engage the science of virtue, and those of us in science engage the church, we can help make the science better. When scientists lean toward the personal health effects of virtues, those in the church can nod and remind them of the larger context of virtues as well. Yes, we may live longer if we forgive our foes, but we will also forge stronger communities and encourage others who observe our forgiveness to forgive their foes as well. We will reflect the forgiveness and grace of a loving God who calls us to accept one another, even as Jesus accepts us (Rom. 15:7). In short, forgiveness is one way we live out the greatest commandments, loving God and neighbor.

Third, the church can be stronger by engaging science in conversation. Even if we in the church know that forgiveness is about more than personal health, we may not know how to go about forgiving very well. But the science can help us. Worthington has offered compelling evidence for his REACH method of forgiveness, discussed in chapter 2, that we can set alongside theological mandates and models until we find ourselves moving toward personal, interpersonal, and community healing. Also, as the church engages in conversation with science, the church remains relevant to coming generations who have learned to trust and accept science, sometimes uncritically. If we Christians can engage science in respectful conversation, then we also gain credibility when it comes to pointing out the limits and weaknesses of scientific methods.

Finally, the science of virtue can help transform the way we understand Christian counseling. So much contemporary counseling is focused on alleviating suffering, and this is a high calling. There will always be a place for weeping with those who weep and comforting those in the most tragic places of life. Counseling is this, but it can also be more. Once the weeping together is done, and the comfort is offered, and trust is established, counselors and clients can together envision a telos. What might it be like to move forward in life toward full functioning and wholeness? Here's an adventure worth considering: maybe Christian counselors, working in the guiding light of God's spirit, can lead the way in bringing virtue back into the counseling office.

Notes

Introduction: A New Conversation about Virtue

1. Christopher Peterson and Martin E. P. Seligman, *Character Strengths and Virtues: A Handbook and Classification* (Washington, DC: American Psychological Association; New York: Oxford University Press, 2004).

2. Alasdair MacIntyre, *After Virtue*, 3rd ed. (Notre Dame, IN: University of Notre Dame Press, 2007).

3. Everett L. Worthington Jr., "What Are the Different Dimensions of Humility?," *Big Questions Online*, November 4, 2014, https://www.bigquestionsonline.com/2014/11/4/what-are-different-dimensions-humility.

4. Paul C. Vitz, *Psychology as Religion: The Cult of Self-Worship*, 2nd ed. (Grand Rapids: Eerdmans, 1995).

5. L. Gregory Jones and Célestin Musekura, *Forgiving as We Have Been Forgiven: Community Practices for Making Peace* (Downers Grove, IL: InterVarsity, 2010).

6. Stanton L. Jones, *Psychology: A Student's Guide* (Wheaton: Crossway, 2014).

Chapter 1 Wisdom

1. Paul McLaughlin and Mark R. McMinn, "Studying Wisdom: Toward a Christian Integrative Perspective," *Journal of Psychology and Theology* 43 (2015): 121–30.

2. Paul B. Baltes and Jacqui Smith, "The Psychology of Wisdom and Its Ontogenesis," in *Wisdom: Its Nature, Origins, and Development*, ed. Robert J. Sternberg (Cambridge: Cambridge University Press, 1990), 94.

3. Robert J. Sternberg, "A Balance Theory of Wisdom," in *The Essential Sternberg*, ed. James C. Kaufman and Elena L. Grigorenko (New York: Springer, 2008), 354.

4. Paul B. Baltes et al., "People Nominated as Wise: A Comparative Study of Wisdom-Related Knowledge," *Psychology and Aging* 10 (1995): 155–66.

5. See, e.g., "Tracing the Bitter Truth of Chocolate and Child Labour," *Panorama*, last updated March 24, 2010, BBC, news.bbc.co.uk/panorama/hi/front _page/newsid_8583000/8583499.stm.

6. Igor Grossmann et al., "Aging and Wisdom: Culture Matters," *Psychological Science* 23 (2012): 1059–66.

7. Monisha Pasupathi, Ursula M. Staudinger, and Paul B. Baltes, "Seeds of Wisdom: Adolescents' Knowledge and Judgment about Difficult Life Problems," *Developmental Psychology* 23 (2004): 351–61.

8. Grossmann et al., "Aging and Wisdom."

9. Ed Diener, Robert Emmons, Randy Larsen, and Sharon Griffin, "The Satisfaction with Life Scale," *Journal of Personality Assessment* 49 (1985): 71–75.

10. Katherine J. Bangen, Thomas W. Meeks, and Dilip V. Jeste, "Defining and Assessing Wisdom: A Review of the Literature," *American Journal of Geriatric Psychiatry* 21 (2013): 1254–66.

11. Lynn G. Underwood and Jeanne A. Teresi, "The Daily Spiritual Experience Scale: Development, Theoretical Description, Reliability, Exploratory Factor Analysis, and Preliminary Construct Validity Using Health-Related Data," *Annals of Behavioral Medicine* 24 (2002): 22–33.

12. Kelly B. Cartwright et al., "Reliability and Validity of the Complex Postformal Thought Questionnaire: Assessing Adults' Cognitive Development," *Journal of Adult Development* 16 (2009): 183–89.

13. Baltes et al., "People Nominated as Wise."

Chapter 2 Forgiveness

1. Charlotte vanOyen Witvliet, Thomas E. Ludwig, and Kelly L. Vander Laan, "Granting Forgiveness or Harboring Grudges: Implications for Emotion, Physiology, and Health," *Psychological Science* 12 (2001): 117–23.

2. Kathleen A. Lawler et al., "A Change of Heart: Cardiovascular Correlates of Forgiveness in Response to Interpersonal Conflict," *Journal of Behavioral Medicine* 26 (2003): 373–93.

3. James W. Carson et al., "Forgiveness and Chronic Low Back Pain: A Preliminary Study Examining the Relationship of Forgiveness to Pain, Anger, and Psychological Distress," *Journal of Pain* 6 (2005): 84–91.

4. Everett L. Worthington Jr. et al., "Forgiveness, Health, and Well-Being: A Review of Evidence for Emotional versus Decisional Forgiveness, Dispositional Forgivingness, and Reduced Unforgiveness," *Journal of Behavioral Medicine* 30 (2007): 291–302.

5. Jennifer Friedberg, Sonia Suchday, and Danielle V. Shelov, "The Impact of Forgiveness on Cardiovascular Reactivity and Recovery," *International Journal of Psychophysiology* 65 (2007): 87–94.

6. Kathleen A. Lawler-Row et al., "Forgiveness, Physiological Reactivity and Health: The Role of Anger," *International Journal of Psychophysiology* 68 (2008): 51–58.

7. Peggy Hannon et al., "The Soothing Effects of Forgiveness on Victims' and Perpetrators' Blood Pressure," *Personal Relationships* 19 (2012): 279–89.

8. Loren Toussaint et al., "Effects of Lifetime Stress Exposure on Mental and Physical Health in Young Adulthood: How Stress Degrades and Forgiveness Protects Health," *Journal of Health Psychology* 21 (2016): 1004–14.

9. Xue Zheng et al., "The Unburdening Effects of Forgiveness," *Social Psychological and Personality Science* 6 (2015): 431–38.

10. Nathaniel G. Wade et al., "Efficacy of Psychotherapeutic Interventions to Promote Forgiveness: A Meta-analysis," *Journal of Consulting and Clinical Psychology* 82 (2014): 154–70.

11. L. Gregory Jones and Célestin Musekura, *Forgiving as We Have Been Forgiven: Community Practices for Making Peace* (Downers Grove, IL: InterVarsity, 2010), 41.

12. Jeremy Taylor, *Holy Living*, updated by Hal M. Helms (Brewster, MA: Paraclete Press, 1988; first published 1650), 57.

13. Alasdair MacIntyre, *After Virtue*, 3rd ed. (Notre Dame, IN: University of Notre Dame Press, 2007).

14. Nathan R. Frise and Mark R. McMinn, "Forgiveness and Reconciliation: The Differing Perspectives of Psychologists and Christian Theologians," *Journal of Psychology and Theology* 38 (2010): 83–90.

15. Jichan Kim and Robert D. Enright, "Why Reconciliation Is Not a Component of Forgiveness: A Response to Frise and McMinn," *Journal of Psychology and Christianity* 34 (2015): 19–25.

16. See Rachel DePompa, "VCU Professor Forgives Killer after Losing His Mother and Brother," *On Your Side*, 2013, NBC 12, http://www.nbc12.com/story/22301562/vcu-professor-forgives-killer-after-losing-his-mother-and-brother.

17. L. Gregory Jones, *Embodying Forgiveness: A Theological Analysis* (Grand Rapids: Eerdmans, 1995).

18. Jones and Musekura, *Forgiving as We Have Been Forgiven*.

19. Jones and Musekura, *Forgiving as We Have Been Forgiven*, 15–33.

20. Everett L. Worthington Jr., *Forgiving and Reconciling: Bridges to Wholeness and Hope* (Downers Grove, IL: InterVarsity, 2003).

21. Jones and Musekura, *Forgiving as We Have Been Forgiven*.

22. Jones and Musekura, *Forgiving as We Have Been Forgiven*, 48.

23. Jones, *Embodying Forgiveness*.

24. Mark R. McMinn et al., "Forgiveness and Prayer," *Journal of Psychology and Christianity* 27 (2008): 101–9.

25. Sarah L. Vasiliauskas and Mark R. McMinn, "The Effects of a Prayer Intervention on the Process of Forgiveness," *Psychology of Religion and Spirituality* 5 (2013): 23–32.

26. Wade et al., "Efficacy of Psychotherapeutic Interventions to Promote Forgiveness."

27. Robert D. Enright, *Forgiveness Is a Choice: A Step-by-Step Process for Resolving Anger and Restoring Hope* (Washington, DC: American Psychological Association, 2001).

Chapter 3 Gratitude

1. Christopher Peterson and Martin E. P. Seligman, *Character Strengths and Virtues: A Handbook and Classification* (Washington, DC: American Psychological Association; New York: Oxford University Press, 2004), 554.

2. Robert Emmons and Michael McCullough, *The Psychology of Gratitude* (New York: Oxford University Press, 2004), 73.

3. Kristján Kristjánsson, "An Aristotelian Virtue of Gratitude," *Topoi* 34 (2015): 499–511.

4. Robert Emmons, *Gratitude Works! A 21-Day Program for Creating Emotional Prosperity* (San Francisco: Jossey-Bass, 2013).

5. Huston Smith and Phil Cousineau, *And Live Rejoicing: Chapters from a Charmed Life* (Novato, CA: New World Library, 2012).

6. Robert A. Emmons and Michael E. McCullough, "Counting Blessings versus Burdens: Experimental Studies of Gratitude and Subjective Well-Being," *Journal of Personality and Social Psychology* 84 (2003): 377–89.

7. Alex M. Wood, Jeffrey J. Froh, and Adam W. A. Geraghty, "Gratitude and Well-Being: A Review and Theoretical Integration," *Clinical Psychology Review* 30 (2010): 890–905.

8. Sara B. Algoe, Barbara L. Fredrickson, and Shelly L. Gable, "The Social Functions of the Emotion of Gratitude via Expression," *Emotion* 13 (2013): 605–9.

9. Amie M. Gordon et al., "To Have and to Hold: Gratitude Promotes Relationship Maintenance in Intimate Bonds," *Journal of Personality and Social Psychology* 103 (2012): 257–74.

10. Paul J. Mills et al., "The Role of Gratitude in Spiritual Well-Being in Asymptomatic Heart Failure Patients," *Spirituality in Clinical Practice* 2 (2015): 5–17.

11. Paul J. Mills, Laura Redwine, and Deepak Chopra, "A Grateful Heart May Be a Healthier Heart," *Spirituality in Clinical Practice* 2 (2015): 24.

12. Don E. Davis et al., "Thankful for the Little Things: A Meta-analysis of Gratitude Interventions," *Journal of Counseling Psychology* 63 (2016): 20–31.

13. Lisa McMinn, *The Contented Soul: The Art of Savoring Life* (Downers Grove, IL: InterVarsity, 2006).

14. Lisa McMinn, *To the Table: A Spirituality of Food, Farming, and Community* (Grand Rapids: Brazos, 2016).

15. Mark R. McMinn, "Flowing like Honey: Gratitude & the Good Life," *Biola University Center for Christian Thought*, July 28, 2014, http://cct.biola.edu/blog/flowing-honey-gratitude-good-life.

16. Davis et al., "Thankful for the Little Things"; Emmons and McCullough, "Counting Blessings versus Burdens."

17. David H. Rosmarin et al., "Maintaining a Grateful Disposition in the Face of Distress: The Role of Religious Coping," *Psychology of Religion and Spirituality* 8 (2015): 134–40.

18. Emmons and McCullough, "Counting Blessings versus Burdens."

19. J. Uhder et al. "A Gratitude Intervention in a Christian Church Community," *Journal of Psychology and Theology* (forthcoming).

Chapter 4 Humility

1. C. S. Lewis, *Mere Christianity* (New York: Macmillan, 1952), 109.

2. Richard J. Foster, *Prayer: Finding the Heart's True Home* (San Francisco: HarperCollins, 1992), 1.

3. David Brooks, *The Road to Character* (New York: Random House, 2015), 5.

4. June Price Tangney, "Humility: Theoretical Perspectives, Empirical Findings and Directions for Future Research," *Journal of Social and Clinical Psychology* 19 (2000): 70–82.

5. Christopher Peterson and Martin E. P. Seligman, *Character Strengths and Virtues: A Handbook and Classification* (Washington, DC: American Psychological Association; New York: Oxford University Press, 2004).

6. Don E. Davis and Joshua N. Hook, "Humility, Religion, and Spirituality: An Endpiece," *Journal of Psychology and Theology* 42 (2014): 111–17.

7. Joshua N. Hook and Don E. Davis, "Humility, Religion, and Spirituality: Introduction to the Special Issue," *Journal of Psychology and Theology* 42 (2014): 3–6.

8. Jennifer E. Farrell et al., "Humility and Relationship Outcomes in Couples: The Mediating Role of Commitment," *Couple and Family Psychology: Research and Practice* 4 (2015): 14–26.

9. Don E. Davis et al., "Humility and the Development and Repair of Social Bonds: Two Longitudinal Studies," *Self and Identity* 12 (2013): 58–77.

10. Pelin Kesibir, "A Quiet Ego Quiets Death Anxiety: Humility as an Existential Anxiety Buffer," *Journal of Personality and Social Psychology* 106 (2014): 610–23.

11. Neal Krause and R. David Hayward, "Humility, Compassion, and Gratitude to God: Assessing the Relationships among Key Religious Virtues," *Psychology of Religion and Spirituality* 7 (2015): 192–204.

12. Joshua B. Grubbs and Julie J. Exline, "Humbling Yourself before God: Humility as a Reliable Predictor of Lower Divine Struggle," *Journal of Psychology and Theology* 42 (2014): 41–49.

13. Caroline R. Lavelock et al., "The Quiet Virtue Speaks: An Intervention to Promote Humility," *Journal of Psychology and Theology* 42 (2014): 99–110.

14. Andrew D. Cuthbert, "Cultivating Humility in Religious Leaders" (PsyD diss., Wheaton College, 2016).

15. Anthony A. Hoekema, *Created in God's Image* (Grand Rapids: Eerdmans, 1994).

16. Andrew Murray, *Humility* (New York: Anson D. F. Randolph & Co., 1895), now in the public domain and available through the website of Ted Hildebrandt, at Gordon College, https://faculty.gordon.edu/hu/bi/ted_hildebrandt /spiritualformation/texts/murray_humility/murray_humility.pdf), 12.

17. Murray, *Humility,* 5.

18. Norman Wirzba, "Food Justice as God's Justice," April 18, 2016, http:// www.tikkun.org/nextgen/food-justice-as-gods-justice.

19. Lisa McMinn, *To the Table: A Spirituality of Food, Farming, and Community* (Grand Rapids: Brazos, 2016).

20. Brooks, *Road to Character*, 9–10.

21. Cuthbert, "Cultivating Humility in Religious Leaders."

22. Lavelock et al., "Quiet Virtue Speaks."

23. Grubbs and Exline, "Humbling Yourself before God."

24. Joshua N. Hook et al., "Cultural Humility: Measuring Openness to Culturally Diverse Clients," *Journal of Counseling Psychology* 60 (2013): 353–66.

25. Joshua J. Knabb, *Faith-Based ACT for Christian Clients: An Integrative Treatment Approach* (New York: Routledge, 2016).

Chapter 5 Hope

1. David Brooks, *The Road to Character* (New York: Random House, 2015), 13–14.

2. Simon S. M. Kwan, "Interrogating Hope: The Pastoral Theology of Hope and Positive Psychology," *International Journal of Practical Theology* 14 (2010): 62.

3. Jürgen Moltmann, *Theology of Hope* (New York: Harper & Row, 1967), 16.

4. Kevin L. Rand and Jennifer S. Cheavens, "Hope Theory," in *The Oxford Handbook of Positive Psychology*, ed. Shane J. Lopez and C. R. Snyder, 2nd ed. (New York: Oxford, 2009), 323–33.

5. Shane J. Lopez, *Making Hope Happen* (New York: Atria Books, 2013).

6. Randy Cohen, Chirag Bavishi, and Alan Rozanski, "Purpose in Life and Its Relationship to All-Cause Mortality and Cardiovascular Events: A Meta-analysis," *Psychosomatic Medicine* 78 (2016): 122–33.

7. Rand and Cheavens, "Hope Theory."

8. Rebecca J. Reichard et al., "Having the Will and Finding the Way: A Review and Meta-analysis of Hope at Work," *Journal of Positive Psychology* 8 (2013): 292–304.

9. Shane J. Lopez, "Making Ripples: How Principals and Teachers Can Spread Hope throughout Our Schools," *Phi Delta Kappan* 92, no. 2 (2010): 40–44.

10. Anthony Scioli and Henry B. Biller, *The Power of Hope: Overcoming Your Most Daunting Life Difficulties—No Matter What* (Deerfield Beach, FL: Health Communications Inc., 2010), 53–54.

11. Anthony Scioli et al., "Hope: Its Nature and Measurement," *Psychology of Religion and Spirituality* 3 (2011): 79.

12. Denise J. Larsen and Rachel Stege, "Client Accounts of Hope in Early Counseling Sessions: A Qualitative Study," *Journal of Counseling & Development* 90 (2012): 45–54.

13. Christopher Peterson and Martin E. P. Seligman, *Character Strengths and Virtues: A Handbook and Classification* (Washington, DC: American Psychological Association; New York: Oxford University Press, 2004), 571.

14. Moltmann, *Theology of Hope*, 33.

15. Mark R. McMinn, *Sin and Grace in Christian Counseling: An Integrative Paradigm* (Downers Grove, IL: InterVarsity, 2008).

16. Barbara B. Taylor, *Speaking of Sin: The Lost Language of Salvation* (Boston: Cowley, 2000), 41.

Chapter 6 Grace

1. John M. G. Barclay, *Paul and the Gift* (Grand Rapids: Eerdmans, 2015).

2. See the Facebook page of Project Amazing Grace, https://www.facebook.com/Project-Amazing-Grace-696913600428471/.

3. Frederick Buechner, *A Room Called Remember: Uncollected Pieces* (San Francisco: HarperCollins, 1984).

4. Mark R. McMinn, *Sin and Grace in Christian Counseling: An Integrative Paradigm* (Downers Grove, IL: InterVarsity, 2008).

5. John Beckenbach, Shawn Patrick, and James N. Sells, "Relationship Conflict and Restoration Model: A Preliminary Exploration of Concepts and Therapeutic Utility," *Contemporary Family Therapy* 32 (2010): 290–301; Shawn Patrick et al., "An Empirical Investigation into Justice, Grace, and Forgiveness: Paths to Relationship Satisfaction," *Family Journal: Counseling and Therapy for Couples and Families* 21 (2013): 142–53.

6. Timothy A. Sisemore et al., "Grace and Christian Psychology—Part 1: Preliminary Measurement, Relationships, and Implications for Practice," *Edification: The Transdisciplinary Journal of Christian Psychology* 4, no. 2 (2011): 57–63; Paul J. Watson, Ronald J. Morris, and Ralph W. Hood Jr., "Sin and Self-Functioning, Part 1: Grace, Guilt, and Self-Consciousness," *Journal of Psychology and Theology* 16 (1988): 254–69.

7. Mark R. McMinn et al., "Professional Psychology and the Doctrines of Sin and Grace: Christian Leaders' Perspectives," *Professional Psychology: Research and Practice* 37 (2006): 295–302.

8. Rodger K. Bufford et al., "Preliminary Analyses of Three Measures of Grace: Can They Be Unified?," *Journal of Psychology and Theology* 43 (2015): 86–97; Rodger K. Bufford, Timothy A. Sisemore, and Amanda M. Blackburn, "Dimensions of Grace: Factor Analysis of Three Grace Scales," *Psychology of Religion and Spirituality* 9 (2017): 56–69.

9. Alan C. Tjeltveit, "Understanding Human Beings in the Light of Grace: The Possibility and Promise of Theology-Informed Psychologies," *Consensus: A Canadian Lutheran Journal of Theology* 29 (2004): 100.

10. Mark R. McMinn, *Why Sin Matters: The Surprising Relationship between Our Sin and God's Grace* (Wheaton: Tyndale House, 2004). See also McMinn, *Sin and Grace in Christian Counseling*.

11. Barbara B. Taylor, *Speaking of Sin: The Lost Language of Salvation* (Boston: Cowley, 2000), 41. See also McMinn, *Why Sin Matters*.

12. See McMinn, *Why Sin Matters*, for a more detailed account.

13. Barclay, *Paul and the Gift*.

14. Jeff A. Moody, "The Effects of a Grace Intervention on a Christian Congregation: A Study of Positive Psychology in the Church" (doctoral dissertation, George Fox University, December 16, 2015).

15. James B. Smith, *The Good and Beautiful God: Falling in Love with the God Jesus Knows* (Downers Grove, IL: InterVarsity, 2009).

16. Laura A. Geczy-Haskins, "The Effects of Grace on Self-Forgiveness within a Religious Community" (doctoral dissertation, George Fox University, October 3, 2016).

17. See Tjeltveit, "Understanding Human Beings in the Light of Grace," for more on this.

18. Anthony A. Hoekema, *Created in God's Image* (Grand Rapids: Eerdmans, 1994).

Conclusion: Let's Work Together

1. David Brooks, *The Road to Character* (New York: Random House, 2015).
2. Russ Harris, *The Happiness Trap* (Boston: Trumpeter, 2011).

3. Joshua J. Knabb, *Faith-Based ACT for Christian Clients: An Integrative Treatment Approach* (New York: Routledge, 2016); Jason A. Nieuwsma, Robyn D. Walser, and Steven C. Hayes, eds., *ACT for Clergy and Pastoral Counselors: Using Acceptance and Commitment Therapy to Bridge Psychological and Spiritual Care* (Oakland, CA: Context Press; New Harbinger Publications, 2016); Timothy A. Sisemore, "Acceptance and Commitment Therapy: A Christian Translation," *Christian Psychology* 8, no. 2 (2014): 5–15.

4. Alasdair MacIntyre, *After Virtue*, 3rd ed. (Notre Dame, IN: University of Notre Dame Press, 2007).

5. Alan C. Tjeltveit, "Understanding Human Beings in the Light of Grace: The Possibility and Promise of Theology-Informed Psychologies," *Consensus: A Canadian Lutheran Journal of Theology* 29 (2004): 100.

Bibliography

Algoe, Sara B., Barbara L. Fredrickson, and Shelly L. Gable. "The Social Functions of the Emotion of Gratitude via Expression." *Emotion* 13 (2013): 605–9.

Baltes, Paul B., and Jacqui Smith. "The Psychology of Wisdom and Its Ontogenesis." In *Wisdom: Its Nature, Origins, and Development*, edited by Robert J. Sternberg, 87–120. Cambridge: Cambridge University Press, 1990.

Baltes, Paul B., Ursula M. Staudinger, Andreas Maercker, and Jacqui Smith. "People Nominated as Wise: A Comparative Study of Wisdom-Related Knowledge." *Psychology and Aging* 10 (1995): 155–66.

Bangen, Katherine J., Thomas W. Meeks, and Dilip V. Jeste. "Defining and Assessing Wisdom: A Review of the Literature." *American Journal of Geriatric Psychiatry* 21 (2013): 1254–66.

Barclay, John M. G. *Paul and the Gift*. Grand Rapids: Eerdmans, 2015.

BBC. "Tracing the Bitter Truth of Chocolate and Child Labour." *Panorama*, last updated March 24, 2010. news.bbc.co.uk/panorama/hi/front_page /newsid_8583000/8583499.stm.

Beckenbach, John, Shawn Patrick, and James N. Sells. "Relationship Conflict and Restoration Model: A Preliminary Exploration of Concepts and Therapeutic Utility." *Contemporary Family Therapy* 32 (2010): 290–301.

Brooks, David. *The Road to Character*. New York: Random House, 2015.

Buechner, Frederick. *A Room Called Remember: Uncollected Pieces*. San Francisco: HarperCollins, 1984.

Bufford, Rodger K., Amanda M. Blackburn, Timothy A. Sisemore, and Rodney L. Bassett. "Preliminary Analyses of Three Measures of Grace: Can They Be Unified?" *Journal of Psychology and Theology* 43 (2015): 86–97.

Bufford, Rodger K., Timothy A. Sisemore, and Amanda M. Blackburn. "Dimensions of Grace: Factor Analysis of Three Grace Scales." *Psychology of Religion and Spirituality* 9 (2017): 56–69.

Carson, James W., Francis J. Keefe, Veeraindar Goli, Anne Marie Fras, Thomas R. Lynch, Steven R. Thorp, and Jennifer L. Buechler. "Forgiveness and Chronic Low Back Pain: A Preliminary Study Examining the Relationship of Forgiveness to Pain, Anger, and Psychological Distress." *Journal of Pain* 6 (2005): 84–91.

Cartwright, Kelly B., Paz Galupo, Seth D. Tyree, and Jennifer G. Jennings. "Reliability and Validity of the Complex Postformal Thought Questionnaire: Assessing Adults' Cognitive Development." *Journal of Adult Development* 16 (2009): 183–89.

Cohen, Randy, Chirag Bavishi, and Alan Rozanski. "Purpose in Life and Its Relationship to All-Cause Mortality and Cardiovascular Events: A Meta-analysis." *Psychosomatic Medicine* 78 (2016): 122–33.

Davis, Don E., Elise Choe, Joel Meyers, Nathaniel Wade, Kristin Varjas, Allison Gifford, Amy Quinn, et al. "Thankful for the Little Things: A Meta-analysis of Gratitude Interventions." *Journal of Counseling Psychology* 63 (2016): 20–31.

Davis, Don E., and Joshua N. Hook. "Humility, Religion, and Spirituality: An Endpiece." *Journal of Psychology and Theology* 42 (2014): 111–17.

Davis, Don E., Joshua N. Hook, Everett L. Worthington Jr., Daryl R. Van Tongeren, Aubrey L. Gartner, David J. Jennings II, and Robert A. Emmons. "Relational Humility: Conceptualizing and Measuring Humility as a Personality Judgment." *Journal of Personality Assessment* 93 (2011): 223–34.

DePompa, Rachel. "VCU Professor Forgives Killer after Losing His Mother and Brother." *On Your Side*, 2013, NBC 12. http://www.nbc12.com/story/22301562 /vcu-professor-forgives-killer-after-losing-his-mother-and-brother.

Diener, Ed, Robert A. Emmons, Randy Larsen, and Sharon Griffin. "The Satisfaction with Life Scale." *Journal of Personality Assessment* 49 (1985): 71–75.

Emmons, Robert A. *Gratitude Works! A 21-Day Program for Creating Emotional Prosperity.* San Francisco: Jossey-Bass, 2013.

Emmons, Robert A., and Michael E. McCullough. "Counting Blessings versus Burdens: Experimental Studies of Gratitude and Subjective Well-Being." *Journal of Personality and Social Psychology* 84 (2003): 377–89.

———. *The Psychology of Gratitude.* New York: Oxford University Press, 2004.

Enright, Robert D. *Forgiveness Is a Choice: A Step-by-Step Process for Resolving Anger and Restoring Hope*. Washington, DC: American Psychological Association, 2001.

Farrell, Jennifer E., Joshua N. Hook, Marciana Ramos, Daryl R. Van Tongeren, Don E. Davis, and John M. Ruiz. "Humility and Relationship Outcomes in Couples: The Mediating Role of Commitment." *Couple and Family Psychology: Research and Practice* 4 (2015): 14–26.

Foster, Richard J. *Prayer: Finding the Heart's True Home*. San Francisco: HarperCollins, 1992.

Friedberg, Jennifer, Sonia Suchday, and Danielle V. Shelov. "The Impact of Forgiveness on Cardiovascular Reactivity and Recovery." *International Journal of Psychophysiology* 65 (2007): 87–94.

Frise, Nathan R., and Mark R. McMinn. "Forgiveness and Reconciliation: The Differing Perspectives of Psychologists and Christian Theologians." *Journal of Psychology and Theology* 38 (2010): 83–90.

Geczy-Haskins, Laura A. "The Effects of Grace on Self-Forgiveness within a Religious Community." Doctoral dissertation, George Fox University, October 2016.

Gordon, Amie M., Emily A. Impett, Aleksandr Kogan, Christopher Oveis, and Dacher Keltner. "To Have and to Hold: Gratitude Promotes Relationship Maintenance in Intimate Bonds." *Journal of Personality and Social Psychology* 103 (2012): 257–74.

Grossmann, Igor, Mayumi Karasawa, Satoko Izumi, Jinkyung Na, Michael Varnum, Shinobu Kitayama, and Richard E. Nisbett. "Aging and Wisdom: Culture Matters." *Psychological Science* 23 (2012): 1059–66.

Grubbs, Joshua B., and Julie J. Exline. "Humbling Yourself before God: Humility as a Reliable Predictor of Lower Divine Struggle." *Journal of Psychology and Theology* 42 (2014): 41–49.

Hannon, Peggy, Eli Finkel, Madoka Kumashiro, and Caryle Rusbult. "The Soothing Effects of Forgiveness on Victims' and Perpetrators' Blood Pressure." *Personal Relationships* 19 (2012): 279–89.

Harris, Russ. *The Happiness Trap*. Boston: Trumpeter, 2011.

Hoekema, Anthony A. *Created in God's Image*. Grand Rapids: Eerdmans, 1994.

Hook, Joshua N., and Don E. Davis. "Humility, Religion, and Spirituality: Introduction to the Special Issue." *Journal of Psychology and Theology* 42 (2014): 3–6.

Hook, Joshua N., Don E. Davis, Jesse Owen, Everett L. Worthington Jr., Shawn O. Utsey, and Terrence Tracey. "Cultural Humility: Measuring

Openness to Culturally Diverse Clients." *Journal of Counseling Psychology* 60 (2013): 353–66.

Jones, L. Gregory. *Embodying Forgiveness: A Theological Analysis*. Grand Rapids: Eerdmans, 1995.

Jones, L. Gregory, and Célestin Musekura. *Forgiving as We Have Been Forgiven: Community Practices for Making Peace*. Downers Grove, IL: InterVarsity, 2010.

Jones, Stanton L. *Psychology: A Student's Guide*. Wheaton: Crossway, 2014.

Kesibir, Pelin. "A Quiet Ego Quiets Death Anxiety: Humility as an Existential Anxiety Buffer." *Journal of Personality and Social Psychology* 106 (2014): 610–23.

Kim, Jichan, and Robert D. Enright. "Why Reconciliation Is Not a Component of Forgiveness: A Response to Frise and McMinn." *Journal of Psychology and Christianity* 34 (2015): 19–25.

Knabb, Joshua J. *Faith-Based ACT for Christian Clients: An Integrative Treatment Approach*. New York: Routledge, 2016.

Koenig, Harold, and Arndt Büssing. "The Duke University Religion Index (DUREL): A Five-Item Measure for Use in Epidemiological Studies." *Religions* 1 (2010): 78–85.

Krause, Neal, and R. David Hayward. "Humility, Compassion, and Gratitude to God: Assessing the Relationships among Key Religious Virtues." *Psychology of Religion and Spirituality* 7 (2015): 192–204.

Kristjánsson, Kristján. "An Aristotelian Virtue of Gratitude." *Topoi* 34 (2015): 499–511.

Kwan, Simon S. M. "Interrogating Hope: The Pastoral Theology of Hope and Positive Psychology." *International Journal of Practical Theology* 14 (2010): 47–67.

Larsen, Denise J., and Rachel Stege. "Client Accounts of Hope in Early Counseling Sessions: A Qualitative Study." *Journal of Counseling & Development* 90 (2012): 45–54.

Lavelock, Caroline R., Everett L. Worthington Jr., Don E. Davis, Brandon J. Griffin, Chelsea A. Reid, Joshua N. Hook, and Daryl R. Van Tongeren. "The Quiet Virtue Speaks: An Intervention to Promote Humility." *Journal of Psychology and Theology* 42 (2014): 99–110.

Lawler, Kathleen A., Jarred W. Younger, Rachel L. Piferi, Eric Billington, Rebecca Jobe, Kim Edmondson, and Warren H. Jones. "A Change of Heart: Cardiovascular Correlates of Forgiveness in Response to Interpersonal Conflict." *Journal of Behavioral Medicine* 26 (2003): 373–93.

Lawler-Row, Kathleen A., Johan C. Karremans, Cynthia Scott, Meirav Edlis-Matityahou, and Laura Edwards. "Forgiveness, Physiological Reactivity and Health: The Role of Anger." *International Journal of Psychophysiology* 68 (2008): 51–58.

Lewis, C. S. *Mere Christianity*. New York: Macmillan, 1952.

Lopez, Shane J. *Making Hope Happen*. New York: Atria Books, 2013.

———. "Making Ripples: How Principals and Teachers Can Spread Hope throughout Our Schools." *Phi Delta Kappan* 92, no. 2 (2010): 40–44.

MacIntyre, Alasdair. *After Virtue*. 3rd ed. Notre Dame, IN: University of Notre Dame Press, 2007.

McElroy, Stacey E., Kenneth G. Rice, Don E. Davis, Joshua N. Hook, Peter C. Hill, Everett L. Worthington Jr., and Daryl R. Van Tongeren. "Intellectual Humility: Scale Development and Theoretical Elaborations in the Context of Religious Leadership." *Journal of Psychology and Theology* 42 (2014): 19–30.

McLaughlin, Paul, and Mark R. McMinn. "Studying Wisdom: Toward a Christian Integrative Perspective." *Journal of Psychology and Theology* (2015): 121–30.

McMinn, Lisa. *The Contented Soul: The Art of Savoring Life*. Downers Grove, IL: InterVarsity, 2006.

———. *To the Table: A Spirituality of Food, Farming, and Community*. Grand Rapids: Brazos, 2016.

McMinn, Mark R. "Flowing like Honey: Gratitude & the Good Life." *The Table* (blog), July 28, 2014. Biola University Center for Christian Thought. http://cct.biola.edu/blog/flowing-honey-gratitude-good-life.

———. *Sin and Grace in Christian Counseling: An Integrative Paradigm*. Downers Grove, IL: InterVarsity, 2008.

———. *Why Sin Matters: The Surprising Relationship between Our Sin and God's Grace*. Wheaton: Tyndale House, 2004.

McMinn, Mark R., Heath Fervida, Keith A. Louwerse, Jennifer L. Pop, Ryan D. Thompson, Bobby L. Trihub, and Susan McLeod-Harrison. "Forgiveness and Prayer." *Journal of Psychology and Christianity* 27 (2008): 101–9.

McMinn, Mark R., Janeil N. Ruiz, David Marx, J. Brooke Wright, and Nicole B. Gilbert. "Professional Psychology and the Doctrines of Sin and Grace: Christian Leaders' Perspectives." *Professional Psychology: Research and Practice* 37 (2006): 295–302.

Mills, Paul J., Laura Redwine, and Deepak Chopra. "A Grateful Heart May Be a Healthier Heart." *Spirituality in Clinical Practice* 2 (2015): 23–24.

186

Bibliography

Mills, Paul J., Laura Redwine, Kathleen Wilson, Meredith A. Pung, Kelly Chinh, Barry H. Greenberg, Ottar Lunde, et al. "The Role of Gratitude in Spiritual Well-Being in Asymptomatic Heart Failure Patients." *Spirituality in Clinical Practice* 2 (2015): 5–17.

Moltmann, Jürgen. *Theology of Hope*. New York: Harper & Row, 1967.

Moody, Jeff A. "The Effects of a Grace Intervention on a Christian Congregation: A Study of Positive Psychology in the Church." Doctoral dissertation, George Fox University, December 2015.

Murray, Andrew. *Humility*. New York: Anson D. F. Randolph & Co., 1895, https://faculty.gordon.edu/hu/bi/ted_hildebrandt/spiritualformation/texts/murray_humility/murray_humility.pdf.

Nieuwsma, Jason A., Robyn D. Walser, and Steven C. Hayes, eds. *ACT for Clergy and Pastoral Counselors: Using Acceptance and Commitment Therapy to Bridge Psychological and Spiritual Care*. Oakland, CA: Context Press/New Harbinger Publications, 2016.

Nouwen, Henri J. M. *The Selfless Way of Christ: Downward Mobility and the Spiritual Life*. London: Orbis, 2007.

Pasupathi, Monisha, Ursula M. Staudinger, and Paul B. Baltes. "Seeds of Wisdom: Adolescents' Knowledge and Judgment about Difficult Life Problems." *Developmental Psychology* 23 (2004): 351–61.

Patrick, Shawn, John Beckenbach, James N. Sells, and Robert F. Reardon. "An Empirical Investigation into Justice, Grace, and Forgiveness: Paths to Relationship Satisfaction." *The Family Journal: Counseling and Therapy for Couples and Families* 21 (2013): 142–53.

Peterson, Christopher, and Martin E. P. Seligman. *Character Strengths and Virtues: A Handbook and Classification*. Washington, DC: American Psychological Association; New York: Oxford University Press, 2004.

Rand, Kevin L., and Jennifer S. Cheavens. "Hope Theory." In *The Oxford Handbook of Positive Psychology*, edited by Shane J. Lopez and Craig R. Snyder, 323–33. 2nd ed. New York: Oxford University Press, 2009.

Reichard, Rebecca J., James B. Avey, Shane Lopez, and Maren Dollwet. "Having the Will and Finding the Way: A Review and Meta-analysis of Hope at Work." *Journal of Positive Psychology* 8 (2013): 292–304.

Rosmarin, David H., Steven Pirutinsky, Devora Greer, and Miriam Korbman. "Maintaining a Grateful Disposition in the Face of Distress: The Role of Religious Coping." *Psychology of Religion and Spirituality* 8 (2015): 134–40.

Scioli, Anthony, and Henry B. Biller. *The Power of Hope: Overcoming Your Most Daunting Life Difficulties—No Matter What*. Deerfield Beach, FL: Health Communications Inc., 2010.

Scioli, Anthony, Michael Ricci, Than Ngugen, and Erica R. Scioli. "Hope: Its Nature and Measurement." *Psychology of Religion and Spirituality* 3 (2011): 78–97.

Sisemore, Timothy A. "Acceptance and Commitment Therapy: A Christian Translation." *Christian Psychology* 8, no. 2 (2014): 5–15.

Sisemore, Timothy A., Matthew Arbuckle, Melinda Killian, Elizabeth Mortellaro, Mahogany Swanson, Robert Fisher, and Joshua McGinnis. "Grace and Christian Psychology—Part 1: Preliminary Measurement, Relationships, and Implications for Practice." *Edification: The Transdisciplinary Journal of Christian Psychology* 4, no. 2 (2011): 57–63.

Smith, Huston, and Phil Cousineau. *And Live Rejoicing: Chapters from a Charmed Life*. Novato, CA: New World Library, 2012.

Smith, James B. *The Good and Beautiful God: Falling in Love with the God Jesus Knows*. Downers Grove, IL: InterVarsity, 2009.

Sternberg, Robert J. "A Balance Theory of Wisdom." In *The Essential Sternberg*, edited by James C. Kaufman and Elena L. Grigorenko, 353–76. New York: Springer, 2008.

Tangney, June Price. "Humility: Theoretical Perspectives, Empirical Findings and Directions for Future Research." *Journal of Social and Clinical Psychology* 19 (2000): 70–82.

Taylor, Barbara B. *Speaking of Sin: The Lost Language of Salvation*. Boston: Cowley, 2000.

Taylor, Jeremy. *Holy Living*. Updated by Hal M. Helms. Brewster, MA: Paraclete Press, 1988. First published 1650.

Thompson, Laura Yamhure, C. R. Snyder, Lesa Hoffman, Scott T. Michael, Heather N. Rasmussen, Laura S. Billings, Laura Heinze, et al. "Dispositional Forgiveness of Self, Others, and Situations." *Journal of Personality* 73 (2005): 313–60.

Tjeltveit, Alan C. "Understanding Human Beings in the Light of Grace: The Possibility and Promise of Theology-Informed Psychologies." *Consensus: A Canadian Lutheran Journal of Theology* 29 (2004): 99–122.

Toussaint, Loren, Grant S. Shields, Gabriel Dorn, and George M. Slavich. "Effects of Lifetime Stress Exposure on Mental and Physical Health in Young Adulthood: How Stress Degrades and Forgiveness Protects Health." *Journal of Health Psychology* 21 (2016): 1004–14.

Uhder, J., M. R. McMinn, R. K. Bufford, and K. Gathercoal. "A Gratitude Intervention in a Christian Church Community." *Journal of Psychology and Theology* (forthcoming).

Underwood, Lynn G., and Jeanne A. Teresi. "The Daily Spiritual Experience Scale: Development, Theoretical Description, Reliability, Exploratory Factor Analysis, and Preliminary Construct Validity Using Health-Related Data." *Annals of Behavioral Medicine* 24 (2002): 22–33.

Vasiliauskas, Sarah L., and Mark R. McMinn. "The Effects of a Prayer Intervention on the Process of Forgiveness." *Psychology of Religion and Spirituality* 5 (2013): 23–32.

Vitz, Paul C. *Psychology as Religion: The Cult of Self-Worship.* 2nd ed. Grand Rapids: Eerdmans, 1995.

Wade, Nathaniel G., William T. Hoyt, Julia E. M. Kidwell, Everett L. Worthington Jr., and Arthur M. Nezu. "Efficacy of Psychotherapeutic Interventions to Promote Forgiveness: A Meta-analysis." *Journal of Consulting and Clinical Psychology* 82 (2014): 154–70.

Watson, Paul J., Ronald J. Morris, and Ralph W. Hood Jr. "Sin and Self-Functioning, Part 1: Grace, Guilt, and Self-Consciousness." *Journal of Psychology and Theology* 16 (1988): 254–69.

Wirzba, Norman. *Food and Faith: A Theology of Eating.* New York: Cambridge University Press, 2011.

———. "Food Justice as God's Justice," April 18, 2016, http://www.tikkun.org/nextgen/food-justice-as-gods-justice.

Witvliet, Charlotte vanOyen, Thomas E. Ludwig, and Kelly L. Vander Laan. "Granting Forgiveness or Harboring Grudges: Implications for Emotion, Physiology, and Health." *Psychological Science* 12 (2001): 117–23.

Wood, Alex M., Jeffrey J. Froh, and Adam W. A. Geraghty. "Gratitude and Well-Being: A Review and Theoretical Integration." *Clinical Psychology Review* 30 (2010): 890–905.

Worthington, Everett L., Jr. *Forgiving and Reconciling: Bridges to Wholeness and Hope.* Downers Grove, IL: InterVarsity, 2003.

———. "What Are the Different Dimensions of Humility?" *Big Questions Online*, November 4, 2014. https://www.bigquestionsonline.com/2014/11/04/what-are-different-dimensions-humility.

Worthington, Everett L., Jr., Charlotte vanOyen Witvliet, Pietro Pietrini, and Andrea J. Miller. "Forgiveness, Health, and Well-Being: A Review of Evidence for Emotional versus Decisional Forgiveness, Dispositional Forgivingness, and Reduced Unforgiveness." *Journal of Behavioral Medicine* 30 (2007): 291–302.

Zheng, Xue, Ryan Fehr, Kenneth Tai, Jayanth Narayanan, and Michele J. Gelfand. "The Unburdening Effects of Forgiveness." *Social Psychological and Personality Science* 6 (2015): 431–38.

Index

absurd contrast, 98–99
Acceptance and Commitment Therapy
    (ACT), 165–66. *See also* counseling,
    Christian
age, wisdom and, 18, 29–36
agency, hope and, 121–22, 131, 137,
    139–40
agriculture. *See* food, humility and
Algoe, Sara, 79
altruism, forgiveness and, 60
anger, 48–50, 62, 117–18
Aristotle, gratitude and, 73–74, 83–84
arrogance, intellectual, 102

back pain, 48–49. *See also* pain
Barclay, John, 150
benefit detection, 85–86
Biller, Henry, 127
blood pressure, 48, 50
Brooks, David, 98–99, 128
busyness, humility and, 97

Carson, James, 48–49
ceiling effect, 90
change, forgiveness and, 63
Christ. *See* Jesus

church, the
    forgiveness and, 51–55, 58–67
    grace and, 146–49, 155–57
    gratitude and, 82–83, 86–92
    hope and, 127–31, 135–39
    humility and, 100, 104–12, 114–18
    science and, 7–9, 167–68
    wisdom and, 20–26, 28–36, 38–39
cognitive model. *See* pathways model
commandments, virtue and, 5–6
commitment, forgiveness and, 60,
    64–65
community, 66–67, 87–90, 107–8,
    137–39. *See also* other, the
contextualism, life-span, 18, 19, 29. *See
    also* wisdom
contrast, absurd, 98–99
conventional wisdom, 21–24, 39–41.
    See also wisdom
costly grace, 144
counseling, Christian
    forgiveness and, 67–69
    grace and, 157–60
    gratitude and, 92–93
    hope and, 139–40
    humility and, 118–20

189

teleology and, 165–66
wisdom and, 39–43
creation, 105, 108–10
critical wisdom, 24–26, 33–36, 38–39, 41–43. *See also* wisdom
crossover design, 87–90
cultural humility, 118
Cuthbert, Andrew, 104, 114–15

Daily Examen, 85
dance steps, forgiveness, 61–63
Davis, Don, 102–3
Davis, Ward, 114–15
decisional forgiveness, 49–50. *See also* forgiveness
deprecation, self, 119–20
depression. *See* deprecation, self
detection, benefit, 85–86
dimensions of grace scale, 144
divine struggle. *See* struggle, divine

efficacy, grace's, 150
Emmons, Robert, 75–78
emotional forgiveness, 49–50. *See also* forgiveness
empathy, 60, 75, 158–59. *See also* other, the
Enright, Robert, 68
eschatology, 123–24
evil, problem of. *See* struggle, divine
Exline, Julie, 117–18

factual knowledge, 17, 19. *See also* knowledge
farming. *See* food, humility and
fear, humility and, 117–18
food, humility and, 109–10
forgiveness
  commitment to, 60, 64–65
  community and, 66
  counseling and, 67–69
  grace and, 151–53, 156
  health and, 48–51
  Jesus and, 52–53, 55–58
  the offender and, 54–55, 61–64, 69
  pain and, 48–49, 59–61
  prayer and, 66–67
  reconciliation and, 55–58, 63, 65, 69
  self and, 7, 52–55, 69
  telos of, 55–58
  types of, 48–51, 152–53
forgivingness. *See* trait forgiveness
fortitude, virtue of, 5

Geczy-Haskins, Laura, 151–54
gifts, 72–73, 83–86, 141–42, 147–48, 150
global humility, 103. *See also* humility
God
  grace and, 142–44, 146, 156
  hope and, 124
  humility and, 105–7
  the other and, 5–6
  See also Jesus
Goetsch, Brian, 135–36
grace
  counseling and, 157–60
  dimensions of, 144, 150
  forgiveness and, 151–53, 156
  God and, 142–44, 146, 156
  gratitude and, 142
  health and, 145
  marriage and, 150–51
  the other and, 144, 156
  patience and, 148–49
  religiosity and, 153–54
  the self and, 144, 147–48, 151–53, 156
  sin and, 155
  telos of, 149–50
  as virtue, 141–44
gratitude
  community and, 86–92
  counseling and, 92–93
  defined, 72
  gifts and, 72–73, 83–86

grace and, 142
health and, 78–81
humility and, 75
Jesus and, 84–85, 92–93
journaling of, 76–77, 79
the other and, 74, 75, 91
practice of, 76–77, 80–85
the self and, 74, 91
telos of, 83–86
as virtue, 73–75
worship and, 87
gratitude fatigue, 76
Grubbs, Joshua, 117–18
guilt, humility and, 117–18

happiness, virtue and, 164–65
healing, Jesus and, 22
health, physical, 48–51, 78–81, 103–4,
    125–27, 145
Hook, Joshua, 102–3
hope
    community and, 137–39
    counseling and, 139–40
    defined, 121–24, 127
    divine struggle and, 121–24, 132–35,
        138, 139–40
    eschatology and, 123–24
    forgiveness and, 63
    health and, 125–27
    Jesus and, 124, 130
    pain and, 125–26, 139–40
    prayer and, 135–36
    the self and, 127–31
    telos of, 131–35
humility
    community and, 107–8, 118
    counseling and, 118–20
    creation and, 105, 108–10
    divine struggle and, 110–12, 117–18
    food and, 109–10
    God and, 105–7
    gratitude and, 75

health and, 103–4
Jesus and, 98–100, 106–7, 112–13
the other and, 101–3, 107–8, 112–13,
    118
pride and, 118–20
the self and, 98–99, 101–3, 110–13,
    116–17, 119–20
submission and, 105–6
superiority and, 103
telos of, 112–13
theology and, 164
types of, 101–3, 108, 118
hypertension, 48, 50

imbalance, forgiveness and, 54–55
incongruity, grace's, 150
informant report, 102
intellectual humility, 102
interventions, gratitude, 80–81
intrinsic religiousness, 153–54

Jesus
    forgiveness and, 52–53, 55–58
    gratitude and, 84–85, 92–93
    hope and, 124, 130
    humility and, 98–100, 106–7, 112–13
    virtue and, 5–6
    wisdom and, 22–26, 38–39
    See also God
Jones, L. Gregory, 59, 61, 62–65
Jones, Stanton, 7
journaling, gratitude, 76–77, 79
justice, virtue of, 5

knowledge, 15–19, 36–38

lament. See struggle, divine
Lavelock, Caroline, 104
Lawler, Kathleen, 48
life satisfaction, 32–33
life-span contextualism, 18, 19. See also
    wisdom
lower back pain, 48–49. See also pain

marriage, grace and, 150–51
McCullough, Michael, 75–78
McElroy, Stacey, 102
meals. *See* food, humility and
mentoring, wisdom and, 30–36
Mills, Paul, 79
Moody, Jeff, 150–51
motivation, forgiveness and, 68
Musekura, Célestin, 59, 61, 62–65

narcissism, 119
nature, 108–10. *See also* creation
neighbor, the. *See* other, the
Newton, John, 148–49
noncircularity, grace's, 150

offender, forgiveness and the, 54–55,
    61–64, 69
openness, intellectual, 102, 108
other, the
    forgiveness and, 54–55, 61–64
    grace and, 144, 156
    gratitude and, 74, 91
    humility and, 101–3, 107–8, 112–13,
        118
    virtue and, 4–7
    See also community; empathy

pain, 48–49, 59–61, 125–26, 139–40.
    See also struggle, divine
paradox, Jesus and, 23
pathways model, 121–22, 131, 137,
    139–40
patience, grace and, 148–49, 159–60
personhood, grace and, 155
positive psychology. *See* science
postformal thought, 33–36. *See also*
    critical wisdom
practical wisdom, 33. *See also* wisdom
pragmatism, wisdom and, 15–16,
    18–24, 33, 39–41
prayer, 66–67, 84–85, 135–36
pride, humility and, 118–20

priority, grace's, 150
procedural knowledge, 17–18, 19. *See
    also* knowledge
prudence, virtue of, 5
psalms, gratitude and, 84

quantification, scientific, 167–68

REACH model, 60
receiving. *See* gifts
reciprocity, grace and, 150
reconciliation, 55–58, 63, 65, 69
relational humility, 103
relativism, values and, 18, 19. *See also*
    wisdom
religiosity, grace and, 153–54

Sabbath, the, 22
sacrilege, Jesus and, 23
satisfaction, life, 32–33
science
    the church and, 7–9, 167–68
    of forgiveness, 46–51, 58–67
    of grace, 144–46, 150–55, 157
    of gratitude, 75–81, 86–92
    of hope, 124–27, 135–39
    of humility, 99–104, 114–18
    quantification and, 167–68
    of wisdom, 15–20, 28–29, 36–39
Scioli, Anthony, 127, 137
self, the
    forgiveness and, 52–55, 69
    grace and, 144, 147–48, 151–53, 156
    gratitude and, 74, 91
    hope and, 127–31
    humility and, 98–99, 101–3, 110–13,
        116–17, 119–20
    virtue and, 4–7
    wisdom and, 16
sin, 23, 63–64, 132–35, 155. *See also*
    struggle, divine
singularity, grace's, 150
skewness, 90

Snyder, C. R., 121
spiritual humility, 108
spirituality, wisdom and, 33–34
state forgiveness, 48, 49, 51, 152–53.
    See also forgiveness
state humility, 101
struggle, divine
    hope and, 121–24, 132–35, 138–40
    humility and, 110–12, 117–18
    virtue and, 164–65
    See also pain; sin
submission, humility and, 105–6
suffering. *See* struggle, divine
superabundance, grace's, 150
superiority, humility and, 103

Tangney, June, 101
teachability, humility and, 101–2
teleology, 26–28, 55–58, 83–86, 112–13,
    131–35, 149–50
temperance, virtue of, 5
theodicy. *See* struggle, divine
theology, humble, 164
trait forgiveness, 48, 49, 51, 152–53. *See
    also* forgiveness

trait humility, 101–3
truth, forgiveness and, 62

Uhder, Jens, 87–90
uncertainty, management of, 18–20. *See
    also* wisdom

values, 18, 19, 166. *See also* wisdom
virtue. *See individual virtues*

Wade, Nathaniel, 68
wisdom
    conventional, 21–24, 39–41
    critical, 24–26, 33–36, 38–39, 41–43
    defined, 15–21
    knowledge and, 15–16, 36–38
    life-span and, 18, 29–36
    as pragmatic, 15–16, 18–24, 33, 39–41
    telos of, 26–28
Witvliet, Charlotte, 48
Wood, Alex, 78–79
worship, gratitude and, 87
Worthington, Everett, 49, 58–60,
    64–65, 68